LINCOLN CHRISTIAN U

W9-BQY-217

FROM THE LIBRARY OF
~~Roger Pedersen~~

Developing
Attitude
Toward
Learning

Robert F. Mager, Ph.D.

FROM THE LIBRARY OF
Roger Pedersen

Fearon Pitman Publishers, Inc.
Belmont, California

For

Albert Bandura,	world's greatest SMATspert;
Maryjane Rees,	magnificent manuscriptor's midwife;
Peter Pipe,	who held my hand from the beginning (making it very difficult to type);
David Cram,	who for the first time is being referred to as Doctor Cram in print;
Ivan Zheesch,	who will never be referred to as Doctor Cram in print; and
Herschel Hirsute,	who is seldom referred to at all.

Copyright © 1968 by Fearon Pitman Publishers, Inc., 6 Davis Drive, Belmont, California 94002. Member of the Pitman Group. All rights reserved. No part of this book may be reproduced by any means, transmitted, or translated into a machine language without written permission from the publisher.

ISBN-0-8224-2000-7

Library of Congress Catalog Card Number: 68-54250

Printed in the United States of America.

Foreword

Robert Mager has written that impossible educational work —a how-to-do-it book that is readable, practical, informative, and enjoyable. And he has done it in that most vexing area of classroom teaching: student attitude toward learning.

I think it will be underlined, asterisked, and dog-eared by professional teachers who want to "produce" students whose future actions will demonstrate how well they have learned, not only by their competency in the subject, but also by their continuing interest in it.

In *Preparing Instructional Objectives*, Dr. Mager stripped away the pedagogical trees hiding the forest of instructional intent. *Developing Attitude Toward Learning* is perhaps the best example yet of "Magerism"—the clarification of complex pedagogy through straightforward language that can be tested in action.

LEON M. LESSINGER
Superintendent
San Mateo (California)
Union High School District

34073

Preface

ONCE UPON A TIME in a little drop of water, King Amoeba decided he wanted to teach his subjects how to have a better life. So he traveled far and wide throughout the Kingdom of Dropland to tell his people how to be better than they were. But nobody listened.

"Psst," said his advisor. "First you have to get their attention. Here. Rub on this magic garlic potion and you will get everyone's attention."

So the king did as he was told and went out to teach his people how to be better than they were. But nobody listened. They swam away . . . and held their noses.

"Psst," said his advisor. "You have to be sure they can hear you. Here. Shout into this megaphone and then everyone will listen."

So the king did as he was told, and went out to spread his wisdom. But nobody listened. They swam away . . . and held their noses . . , and covered their ears.

"Psst," said his advisor. "The people are too stupid to realize what wisdom you have to offer. You have to *make* them listen for their *own good*."

So the king made everyone gather in the Great Solarium while he told them how to be better than they were. But when the Great Doors were opened, everybody swam away so hard and so fast that before they knew it they had swum right out of Dropland. And henceforth and forevermore they were referred to as Outdroppers.

And the moral of this fable is that . . . *things surrounded by unpleasantness are seldom surrounded by people.*

There is no question that what we *teach* is often different from what we *tell*. Sometimes we teach the beauty and importance of a subject as well as the substance of it. Sometimes though, we teach people to dislike, and then to avoid, the very subject we are teaching them about.

Developing Attitude Toward Learning is about a universal objective of instruction—the intent to send students away from instruction with at least as favorable an attitude toward the subjects taught as they had when they first arrived. It is about the conditions that influence this attitude, about how to recognize it, and about how to evaluate it.

This book is *not* about what to teach. It is simply about a way to help students get the best use of what they have been taught, and about how to influence them to learn more about your favorite subject after they have left you.

If you do not care whether your students use what you have taken the trouble to teach them, this book is not for you

ROBERT F. MAGEP

There once was a teacher
Whose principal feature
Was hidden in quite an odd way.
    Students by millions
    Or possibly zillions
    Surrounded him all of the day.

When finally seen
By his scholarly dean
And asked how he managed the deed,
    He lifted three fingers
    And said, "All you swingers
    Need only to follow my lead.

"To rise from a zero
To Big Campus Hero,
To answer these questions you'll strive:
    Where am I going,
    How shall I get there, and
    How will I know I've arrived?"

Contents

Where Am I Going?

A thing, to be useful, has got to be used
But hated things, sir, are less used than abused.

1

What It's All About

People influence people. Since you are people, then *you*
influence people. That's clear enough. But do you know just
how you influence people? Do you know that you can have a
great deal of control over the favorability of your influence?

That's what this book is all about. It is about some of the
principles you can apply to influence your students' attitudes
positively, about how you can find out how well you are doing,
and about how you can find out how to do better. The sole
intent is to aid in sending students away from your instruction
anxious to use what you have taught them—and eager to learn
more.*

*If you understand how favorable attitudes, approach tendencies, and the
inclination to use that which is learned are related—if you are ready to plunge
right into a consideration of how to increase the strength of an attitude toward
the subject you teach—turn directly to Chapter 4, page 21.

3

Let's begin with a story.

A small boy of nine once looked forward to beginning his study of the violin. He admired his father, who played happy tunes on the violin, and he enjoyed music. His friends were studying various musical instruments, and he eagerly awaited the day he could call himself a musician. The day finally arrived, and, tucking his new violin under his arm, he started out toward an entirely new experience in learning.

What happened then? How did the story turn out?

A story like this could end in many ways. The boy might become a great violinist, enchanting millions with his skill. Or, lacking the talent of the virtuoso, he might become a very good violinist in a symphony orchestra. With even less talent, but continued interest, he might instead come to play the violin as a pleasurable hobby, providing enjoyment for himself and his friends.

On the other hand, he might come to hate the sound of the violin—perhaps even music itself—even with the talent to develop considerable skill.

Exactly how the story of an experience with an object or an activity *does* end is the result of the things that happen to a person while he is in the presence of that object or activity. The history of an attitude toward a subject is influenced by the events that occur in relation to it.

In the case of our small boy, the end of the story happens to be disappointing. Though he didn't have the talent to become a great violinist, he could, and did, make sufficient progress during four years of effort to enable him to make some very pleasant sounds. But alas, at that point he gave up the violin entirely and never played it again.

Why?

Surely *many* events could have influenced the gradual shaping of his attitude from positive to negative; *many* circumstances could have been responsible for the gradual strangulation of a willingness to learn and to use what had been learned. It may have been that the boy's friends made fun of him. It may have been the fact that the window of his "practicing" room faced the neighborhood baseball field, or that the violin was used as an instrument of punishment ("You didn't come when I called you, so you have to practice an extra half hour"). It may even have been his teacher. Perhaps the teacher appeared continually angry at having to work with a "beginner"; perhaps he showed nothing but dissatisfaction with the progress of his student. Perhaps he always expected more than the boy could give. Or perhaps he ridiculed or insulted his student, or in some other way turned himself into a thing to be feared.

Suppose our student had had a phenomenal talent for the violin. Would talent *alone* have assured an attitude favorable to continued association with the instrument? Would the student's talent have reached fruition even in the face of repeated ridicule, distractions, insensitive teaching, or constant punishment? Perhaps . . . and perhaps not. Although we may never know how a given individual might have behaved under a different set of circumstances, it is clear that circumstances *do* influence behavior—both favorably and unfavorably.

Where Are We Heading?

One of the important goals of teaching is to prepare the student to *use* the skills and knowledge he has learned and to prepare him to *learn more* about the subjects he has been taught. One way of reaching this goal is to send the student away from the learning experience with a tendency to approach, rather than avoid, the subject of study. The remainder of this book is designed to help you achieve this objective.

If telling were the same as teaching, we'd all be so smart we could hardly stand it.

2

Why It's All About

Why do we teach?

Why do we decide to construct a "course of instruction"?

What do we hope to achieve?

We teach or instruct because we hope that through our instruction the student will somehow be different than he was before the instruction. We provide "learning experiences" with the intent that the student will then be a modified person . . . in knowledge, in attitude, in belief, in skill.

We teach in order to influence the capabilities of the student.

Consider any of the instruction you yourself may have given. Why did you lecture, or tutor, or otherwise assist the student to learn? Wasn't it because you hoped he would, as a result of your efforts,

- Know more than he knew before,
- Understand something he did not understand before,
- Develop a skill that was not developed before,
- Feel differently about a subject than he felt before, or
- Develop an appreciation for something where there was none before?

If your intent *was* to achieve one or more of these results, then it was in these same ways that you hoped the student would become different than he was before the instruction.

Many words are used to describe these intended differences. We talk about developing skills, or competencies, or attitudes, or enthusiasm. We talk about encouraging growth or self-actualization, about helping the student to develop, or about assisting him to develop to his fullest potential. Regardless of the words we use to describe our teaching goals, and regardless of the goals, *no teaching goal can be reached unless the student is influenced to become different in some way than he was before the instruction was undertaken.*

Equally important to reaching a teaching goal is timing— *when* do we want the differences to appear?

Do we teach algebra, or reading, or logic so that the student can perform these skills *now,* without any concern for the future? When we attempt to impart an appreciation for music, are we only concerned that the appreciation be done *during* the course, during the period of our influence?

No. We are far more concerned with influencing how the student is able to perform *after* the course is over, *after* our influence is discontinued. We try to instill an appreciation for music *now* so that the student will behave appreciatively *after* our help has been withdrawn. We try to teach him to read *now* so that he will be able to read well in the *future*. And whether we are concerned with his performance in the immediate future or in the more remote future, we are concerned that our teaching influence become at least as evident *then* as we want it to become evident *now*.

Dr. Jerome Bruner summarized the point exceedingly well: "The first object of any act of learning . . . is that it should serve us in the future."*

Certainly one of the important goals of education is that the influence of an educational experience will extend beyond the period of instruction. This goal is implied in almost every statement of educational objectives.

There is no concern at this point with whether any particular goal can be achieved through formal education, with whether it ought to be achieved, or even with whether it is stated in a way that facilitates achievement. The concern is only with noting that the actions implied by the educational goals are expected to be performable at some time subsequent to the instruction—*at some time after the direct influence of the instructor has ended.*

There is nothing new about saying we are interested in having students use what we have taught them after instruction has ended. The point may seem belabored, but if this goal is worth achieving, it is a goal worth doing more about than just talking. If it is an objective of value, we must act to achieve it, and act to learn how well we succeed.

If it's worth teaching, isn't it worth knowing if we have succeeded?

Suppose it *is* true that instruction is intended to facilitate performance at some time after the instruction has taken place, you might ask. So what?

Just this. The more important what you have to teach your students is, the more important it is that they be willing to *use* what you have taught them. If you go to

---

*Jerome S. Bruner, *The Process of Education*, Cambridge, Mass.: Harvard University Press, 1960, p. 17.

the great trouble of putting your own thoughts in order and organizing effective learning experiences for your students, you should certainly want to avoid the state of affairs implied by a graduate who says, "Boy, I hope I never hear of *that* subject again." What a waste that would be—of your talents and of the student's talents. You would have wasted *your* talents teaching him something important that he will probably never use. He would have wasted *his* talents learning (and then not using) a skill or knowledge that might have enabled him to be a little more successful, a little more useful, a little happier, or a little greater.

If it's worth teaching, isn't it worth working toward having that teaching put to use?

If one of our goals is to influence the student to think about, learn about, talk about, and *do something about* our subject some time after our direct influence over him comes to an end, how can we say we have been successful if the student actively avoids any further mention of the subject?

Whatever else we do in the way of influencing the student, the *least* we must strive to achieve is to send him away with favorable rather than unfavorable feelings about the subject or activity we teach. This might well be our minimum, and universal, goal in teaching.

(Of course, it isn't necessary for people to "like" a subject or activity in order for them to come into contact with it, or use it, or do something about it. Look at all the things people do that they would rather not do. Add up the time you spend doing things not of *your* choice. But this is just the point. People try to spend as much time as possible doing those things that they feel favorably about, and they avoid doing those things they feel unfavorably about . . . except when circumstances *prevent* them from doing so. Those who dread the thought of mathematics, for example, will struggle with some calculations . . . when they have to. Those who can't stand operatic music will sit through it . . . when there is no choice. When there *is* a choice, the ex-student will be more likely to apply what we have taught him if he is favorably disposed toward the subject than if he hates the mention of it. And there *are* things we can do to accentuate the positive and eliminate the negative.)

Teachers, of course, don't control *all* of the factors that influence a student's attitude. There are parents, there are peers, and there is the neighborhood There is the uncle he has always admired, and there are the mass media. Therefore, we must be realistic in our expectations.

But if you agree that there are several factors not under a teacher's control that influence behavior *toward* or *away from* a subject, you must also agree that attitude *can* be influenced, and that if *other* people influence, *you* influence. Put another way, although it is true the teacher doesn't control *all* the factors that influence behavior toward or away from a subject, this does not alter the fact that the teacher is *one* of the influencing factors.

Let me summarize what has been discussed this far.

- Learning is for the *future*; that is, the object of instruction is to facilitate some form of behavior at a point *after* the instruction has been completed.

- The likelihood of the student putting his knowledge to use is influenced by his *attitude* for or against the subject; things disliked have a way of being forgotten.

- People influence people. Teachers, and others, *do* influence attitudes toward subject matter—and toward learning itself.

- One objective toward which to strive is that of having the student leave your influence with as *favorable* an attitude toward your subject as possible. In this way you will help to maximize the possibility that he will *remember* what he has been taught, and will willingly *learn more* about what he has been taught.

How to proceed? What can you actually *do* to enable you to claim you have done your best toward the achievement of the objective of having the student leave your influence with as favorable an attitude toward your subject as possible?

Perhaps the best way to begin is to clarify the objective, and then identify the kinds of things a student might be *seen doing* if the objective were achieved. Following that, try to identify some of the practices that would *help achievement* of the objective. Finally, explore available procedures for checking your instruction to see if you have inadvertently allowed any hindering conditions to exist, and to see which helping conditions might be added to those you are already using.

Much remains to be learned, however, and I am not pretending to present a final answer to a very important question. But a great deal is already known about human behavior, and our instructional power will be increased to the extent this knowledge is understood and put into practice.

If you're not sure where you're going, you're liable to end up someplace else.

3

Developing the Objective

Although objectives such as teaching students "to appreciate" music or "to acquire a respect for" the American judiciary system may be laudable, they are difficult, if not impossible, to achieve when stated only in such vague terms.

For an instructional objective to be useful it must be stated in concrete terms. Ideally, it will identify what a student would be doing when demonstrating his achievement of the objective, suggest conditions relevant to the desired performance, and suggest how to tell when the objective has been achieved.

A usefully stated objective, in other words, is one that helps us to see where we are heading and tells us how to know when we have arrived.

Since you may not as yet have dangled your mind's toe in the murky waters of affective objectives (those having to do with feelings or attitude), and since this area is populated more by good intentions than by knowledge and experience, it will be best to proceed with caution.

The first step is to consider the word "attitude." Though "attitude" is a useful word in everyday conversation, and I have used it myself so far in this book, it is about as useful as a bikini in the Arctic when we are concerned with objectives we seriously intend to achieve.

There is no *thing* inside us called an attitude, not in the sense that there is something inside us called a heart. You couldn't dissect someone with a positive attitude toward hamburgers and find it (the attitude, that is) any more than you could dissect him and find a laugh.

Actually, "attitude" is a word used to refer to a *general tendency* of an individual to act in a certain way under certain conditions.

Our use of the word "attitude" is based on what someone says or what he does. *It is based on visible behavior.*

For example, when we note that a person tends to say "bleaugh!" every time he is faced with an avocado, we might say he doesn't like avocados. When we make such an observation, we are making an inference from visible behavior about an internal, invisible condition.

A good friend of mine has a favorable attitude toward Bach; that is, he likes to listen to music written by Bach. Now this statement is an inference on my part about a tendency, inclination, propensity—or "attitude." It is a conclusion about a general state of affairs based on circumstantial evidence. What kind of circumstantial evidence? Well, he talks about Bach whenever he can slip him into a conversation, and he frequently locates himself where the music of Bach is being played. And he does this for no reason at all . . . by which I mean there is no observable coercion—no visible or audible Bach stimuli to prod him. He simply makes numerous "moving toward" responses to Bach's music. So, from my observations I infer that he has a positive attitude toward Bach.

Whenever we use the word "attitude," we are making a prediction about the future behavior of a person based on our observations of his past behavior.

If we say a person has a *favorable attitude* toward classical music, it means we predict he will say favorable things about it, that he will put himself into the presence of that kind of stimulus, and that he will stay in the presence of that kind of stimulus as long as he can.

If we say that a person has a *negative attitude* toward television, it means we are predicting that if he is put into the presence of a TV set he will try to get away as best he can, and that he is not likely to bestir himself very often to put himself into the presence of that kind of stimulus.

When we tag someone as having a "favorable attitude," we are predicting some form of *moving toward* responses, and this prediction is based on some "moving toward" behavior already seen. Conversely, tagging a person as having a "negative attitude" is predicting *moving away from* responses, and that prediction is based on some "moving away from" behavior already observed.

Suppose we talk about **behavior** instead of "attitude." After all, it is the behavior of the student with which we are concerned. By limiting ourselves to behavior, we skirt the nebulous realm of "reallys"—whether a student "really" has this kind of attitude or that kind of attitude. In behavior, we have something concrete; we are dealing with responses. We can concentrate on increasing the incidence of "moving toward," or *approach* responses, and reducing the incidence of "moving away from," or *avoidance* responses. We can not only aim for an objective and act to achieve it, but we can *evaluate our success in achieving the objective.*

Having tabled the term "attitude" in favor of something more manageable, we can now state the objective:

> At the end of my influence over the student, when in the presence of the subject of_____, the percentage of approach responses made by him will be at least as great as it was when the student first arrived.

Does this objective tell what to look for in the way of student behavior?

Yes. It asks for *approach responses toward the subject.*

Does the objective tell when the behavior is expected to appear?

Yes. It says the behavior is expected to appear *when the student is about to leave your influence.* The behavior might appear some time before he leaves, of course, and you may want to sample approach tendency at regular intervals to see how, and whether, it is moving in a positive direction. The essential point is that the desired performance be observed before the student disappears over the horizon.

The objective also indicates that you will have to make an assessment when the student arrives as well as just before he leaves, suggesting that a before-and-after comparison must be made. The wording of the objective indicates that it doesn't matter which test items or situational items you use to evaluate the approach tendency; the important thing is that the percentage of approach responses at the end of your influence be at least as high as it was at the beginning of your influence. (Just what kinds of test items and situational items might be useful will be taken up later.)

Some people may wonder why the objective only talks about what the student does when *presented with* the subject matter and not about the frequency of occasions on which he might *put himself* into the presence of the subject matter. After all, aren't we interested in more than approach responses that occur when the student just happens to be faced with the subject or activity?

Of course we are. But if you are interested in how the student responds in relation to your subject *after* he has left you, that intent warrants a separate statement, for it is a different objective. A suitable statement of that objective might be as follows:

During the period extending from_____to_____,
the frequency of approach responses of the student to
the subject of _____ will be at least as great
as it was during the first month of influence.

Assuming that students are available to you after they have
left your direct influence, how might you measure the achievement of this objective? You could follow them around and
count the number of times they did something in relation to the
subject you taught them. Pretty clearly, that isn't very practical.
Instead, you could ask *them* to keep track of the number of
times they did something in relation to your subject; that is, you
could ask them to keep track of the number of records they
bought, concerts they attended, number of times they painted
a picture, amount of time they spent solving math problems,
and so on. Unless it is practical to assess student performance
after instruction has ended, however, it is best to confine an
objective to that which can be achieved during your period of
influence over the student; that way you will always be able to
measure your success at achieving that which you intend. It is
for this reason that the objective on page 15 is preferred.

Since achievement of the objective involves influencing the
tendency to approach, now is the time to consider just what an
approach behavior is and how to recognize one when you see
one.

How Shall
I Get There?

A teacher with insight once turned
To a colleague and said, "I've discerned
That if I'm aversive
While waxing discursive
My students detest what they've learned."

4

Recognizing Approach

Can you recognize an approach response when you see one?

An approach response, you'll recall, is an action that indicates a *moving toward* the subject (an object, activity, or situation) about which you are interested in making a tendency statement. It is a behavior that results in contact with the target subject or in moving closer to the target subject, or which leads you to conclude that moving closer would be likely under appropriate circumstances.

For example, when my wife serves me a plate of steak, I eat it. This is an approach response plus. My behavior not only moves me closer to the target subject, it moves me to surround it (closer than which I cannot get). If, on the other hand, my wife serves me a plate of spinach or limp green beans, I push my plate away. Since this behavior moves me farther from the target subject, it can be labelled an avoidance behavior. It is unnecessary to get all tangled up in concern over whether this means I "like" or "dislike" the items in question. If I move toward the subject, I am making an approach response; if I move the subject away from me, or vice versa, I am making an avoidance response. That's all.

Suppose you heard this dialogue.

"Ahh, kiss me, you fool."
    "Thank you, but I'd rather not."
"Why not?"
    "I never kiss on Wednesdays."

It seems fairly obvious that the second speaker is trying to move away from the first speaker. This an an avoidance response, even though it is verbal. Again, it does not matter *why* the behavior occurred. It doesn't matter whether it was because the first speaker suffered from bad breath or from crumpled toes. It doesn't matter whether it had anything to do with the attraction, or lack of it, of the second speaker for the first. If the response was "moving away from" behavior, it was an avoidance response.

How can you identify a variety of behaviors that indicate approach responses?

You might well begin by observing a few people who clearly have strong approach tendencies toward particular activities. What is it they do that leads you to such conclusions?

First, take a close look at a baseball fan. I'm sure you will agree that a baseball fan has strong approach tendencies toward the subject and the activity of baseball.

What tells you he likes baseball? What does he *do* that causes you to reach the conclusion that "he sure is a nut about baseball"?

Suppose you were to observe such a person for a week, and suppose you were to record in your notebook everything he did that you consider evidence of his liking for baseball. At the end of the week, your notes might read something like this:

—— Talks incessantly about baseball.

—— Reads every word about the subject printed on the sports pages of both local newspapers.

—— Can recite the batting averages of all players of all teams in both leagues.

—— During the observation week, watched every game telecast.

—— On Tuesday and Thursday, risked losing his job by calling in sick in order to attend doubleheaders.

This list by no means exhausts the possibilities. You will be astonished at the number of approach responses you will find once you begin to look for them. Just a month or two ago, I ran into an excellent example of approach response toward this very subject. In a letter to one of the personal advice columns of the Chicago *Daily News*, a woman wrote:

I know men are crazy about sports, but my husband carries this too far. He even took a transistor radio to his sister's wedding so he wouldn't miss the baseball game.

Clearly this man's behavior caused him to come closer to, or to remain in contact longer with, the subject of baseball; it is an approach response.

Next, consider the person who is known as an "opera enthusiast." If you were to observe and record his behavior for a while to see what might have led to this description of him, your notes might look something like this:

—— Attends all local operas, regardless of cost.

—— Talks about opera at length whenever possible.

—— Tells nonenthusiasts that they "just don't know what they are missing."

——— Reads books about opera.

——— Frequently hums arias from various operas.

——— Subscribes to an opera magazine.

——— Owns an extensive record collection of favorite operas.

Again, the list of responses that represent an attempt to approach or remain in contact with opera has not been exhausted. Can you think of others?

Now, look for approach responses in an area more closely related to instruction. Here's a fellow currently enrolled in the second semester of a college biology course. His instructor is frequently referred to as "enthusiastic," "inspiring," and "a good teacher." But you don't want to ask about the behavior of the instructor at this point. You are interested in the behavior of the student; more specifically, in discovering evidence from which to predict the nature of this student's future behavior toward the subject of biology. A week-long observation of this student might reveal the following:

——— During the week, student went to the library twelve times; spent 70 per cent of his time there reading biology books.

——— Tuesday evening, student attended meeting of the university biology club; broke date with favorite girl to attend.

——— Wednesday morning, spent $10.00 on biology texts, $7.50 on dissecting instruments.

——— Survey of attendance records shows that student has never missed a biology lecture or laboratory, although he has cut two or three classes in each of his other college courses.

——— During the week's three lectures and two laboratory periods, student asked 14 questions, all related to biology.

——— Asked to see his instructor twice in his office to discuss points not covered in course.

—— On Thursday, student crouched on the banks of a river for three predawn hours to capture frogs for use as specimens.

—— Student visited his advisor to ask if he could register for an advanced biology course.

You may object that this list contains exaggerations or that there are omissions, and you may not be willing to accept all the items as relevant to your own situation, but you will surely agree that it contains responses that can be used to make predictions (statements of approach or avoidance tendencies) about the student's future behavior toward biology.

As you can see by these examples, people who are strongly disposed toward a subject talk a great deal about it, encourage others to participate in it, read about it, buy books about it, attend lectures about it, publish papers about it, and enter careers about it. Students strongly disposed toward a subject sign up for more courses about it, say favorable things about it, and spend their study time studying it.

In general, then, we can say that people with strong approach tendencies toward a subject keep coming back for more experiences with the subject. They seek out experiences with the subject in preference to other desirable experiences. *The more strongly they are attracted to a subject, the more obstacles they will overcome to come into contact with it and stay in contact with it.**

As you are well aware, an approach response can be "faked," and it can be coerced. A person might express an interest in a subject, or work with it, under some circumstances and not under others. As long as you know that this can be the case, you will be all right. The important thing is to be able to recognize the difference between an approach response and an *interpretation* of that response. First find the responses, and then weigh them.

---

*One of the most interesting examples of an approach response was this classified advertisement brought to my attention by Peter Pipe.

WANTED: Someone who watches *Love of Life* to fill in an episode missed.

The confidence with which weight can be put on approach responses is related to your knowledge of the circumstances under which the responses were made. Little or no weight can be put on responses made under conditions where the person is reacting to stimuli *other* than the one you want to evaluate. This is exactly how you would evaluate responses to items on a subject matter test. For example, if you knew that a student used a crib sheet while responding to a series of physics questions, you would consider his responses less indicative of the state of his physics knowledge than if the responses were made under circumstances devoid of such illegal assistance.

Approach tendencies, however, are only half the story. There are also subjects that some people tend to avoid. If we can identify responses that lead us to conclude that a person tends toward a subject, we should also be able to identify responses indicating a person's tendency away from a subject.

Had you been observing and recording my behavior when I sat down to complete the third revision of this chapter, your notes might have looked something like this:

—— Sat down and turned on electric typewriter.

—— Turned off electric typewriter.

—— Went to kitchen for a cup of coffee.

—— Rearranged papers on desk and sharpened pencils.

—— Looked out window to check smog level.

—— Sat down and turned on electric typewriter.

—— Inspected fingernails.

—— Turned off electric typewriter.

—— Went to get nail file.

—— Filed nails.

It wouldn't really matter what responses you might have seen me make. If the result was to take me farther away from the typewriter, you would have been correct to label them avoidance responses.

There are some subjects that may be avoided by people who actually "like" them very much. A fat man, for example, might manage to say "No, thank you" when offered his favorite dish, or a woman might avoid buying a hat that she wants very much. These are special cases where a person avoids a subject because by doing so he avoids an aversive (undesirable or disagreeable) consequence: the fat man avoids getting fatter, more uncomfortable, and, possibly, some stern comments from his physician; the woman hankering after the hat avoids getting thrown out of the house by her husband.

But what about matters closer to home—actions that might be used to infer an avoidance tendency toward an academic subject? The record of a student in his second semester of a required college mathematics course might look like this:

- —— On Tuesday, student tried to convince mathematics instructor that he should excuse him from the course.
- —— Failed to turn in three of four mathematics assignments on time.
- —— Wednesday, he spoke with his advisor about dropping out of the mathematics course.
- —— Monday and Wednesday, he was late for mathematics class; on Friday, he failed to appear.
- —— Discussion with instructor of first semester mathematics course revealed that student did not have the prerequisites necessary for the course and that he frequently complained mathematics was unrelated to reality; instructor had evidence the student did very little studying.
- —— Discussion with student revealed that he is convinced he has no aptitude for mathematics, cannot learn anything about mathematics, will never need mathematics, and would be content if he never heard the subject mentioned again.

There are other responses that can be considered as evidence of the existence of an avoidance tendency. Some people who dislike a subject or activity say unfavorable things about it, thereby influencing others toward an avoidance tendency; some go to great lengths to discourage others from experiencing the subject, signing up for a course, listening to a discussion, or participating in relevant activities.*

Given a choice, people with avoidance tendencies elect to approach something other than the subject in question. They will go to varying lengths to prevent contact with the subject. They do not buy or read books about the subject, they do not join clubs relating to the subject, and they do not seek out discussions concerning the subject. When they are faced with the subject, they act to move away from it by changing the topic of conversation, by walking away from the stimulus, or by inventing an excuse to avoid the subject or terminate contact with it.

More importantly, in instructional situations, people often verbalize a conviction that they cannot learn a particular subject matter and that they intend to have as little as possible to do with the subject in the future. *Once such a behavior pattern develops, it is unlikely that it will be reversed.*

To the extent the student avoids experiences with the subject, he will have fewer opportunities to change his avoidance tendency to an approach tendency. In addition, if a student avoids experiences with a subject, it is improbable that he will use and maintain whatever skill he might have, and it is almost certain that he will learn little more about it as time goes by. Each sub-

---

*I had an opportunity to witness an hilarious set of avoidance behaviors when I first suggested a title for this book to the publisher. Since the book was to be about Subject Matter Approach Tendencies and Subject Matter Unapproach Tendencies, I suggested we call the work "SMATs 'n SMUTs."

Now publishers have to put up with all sorts of unusual behavior on the part of authors, and they learn to cope with most of it. So when I gave them my title suggestion, the first reaction was the polite chuckle . . . which said, "There, there, now (pat, pat) that's a nice little joke . . . but you aren't *serious?*"

When I persisted in suggesting that it had just the right sort of zing to it, the next subtle avoidance response was, "Well, let's see if it fits after we've worked over the rest of it," still hoping it would go away.

Seeing me persistent yet, they launched into a heart-rending discussion of the Fanny Hill implications of the title, and of how publishers had people on their staff with a "feel" for titles. Eventually I gave up, but not before being impressed once again with the great variety of behaviors that are indicative of avoidance.

ject a student avoids constitutes the loss of a tool or skill that might have eased his journey through a complex world.

It is for this reason that instruction that produces subject matter avoidance tendencies may very well do the student more harm than good.

(That good intentions are not enough was clearly demonstrated by an approach-avoidance analysis recently conducted for a high school teacher of mathematics. This teacher is highly motivated to generate enthusiasm and appreciation for mathematics in her students. She likes what she teaches and is anxious that her students share her excitement for the subject. She is courteous and respectful of student questions, and makes herself available for questions.

But in spite of her intentions and her initial success at motivation, she managed to *reduce* math interest in about as many students as she managed to increase it.

How? What could such a teacher be doing to diminish subject matter approach tendencies?

It was a classic example of "overkill." She inadvertently spent a great deal of class time presenting material beyond the ability of her students to understand. Her enthusiasm for her subject caused her to try to teach almost everything she knew about math, and that was a lot more than students could understand, regardless of how motivated they were to try. Some students concluded that they could never understand math, and lost interest.)

These three procedures will help you to improve your ability to pinpoint approach and avoidance responses:

1. Think of the likes and dislikes of a friend, and then ask yourself what he *does* or *says* that leads you to make such classifications.

2. When you hear someone comment on the likes, dislikes, or attitudes of another, ask him what that person *says* or *does* that causes him to make that comment.

3. If you are an instructor, carry a small notebook with you and note each event that leads you to believe a student is either favorably or unfavorably disposed toward a subject (never does his homework, sleeps in class, doesn't pay attention, always carries the textbook, talks incessantly about the subject, gets so absorbed in assignment he can't hear his name called, etc.).

Approach and avoidance responses are the raw materials from which we make predictions about future behavior; they are the circumstantial evidence from which we make statements about tendencies. Though the quality of these statements depends on the quality of our evidence, the fact remains that there is *tangible* evidence from which reliable statements about attitudes can be made. We do not have to rely on faith or intuition in the matter of achieving our over-all instructional objective. *We can act to develop and strengthen approach tendencies toward our subject of instruction and we can find out whether we have succeeded.*

If our actions didn't sometimes shout louder than our words, there would be no call for the expression, "Don't do as I do, do as I say."

5

Sources of Influence

Not very long ago, Von Haney, a talented graphic artist, created a short animation sequence for an instructional program designed to teach the average American housewife something about the principles of behavior so that she might increase her success at interaction with those around her. In this sequence, there are two small boys, one empty-handed and the other holding and sucking a huge lollipop. The empty-handed boy speaks first:

"Hi. Where'd you get the sucker?"

"My mommy gave it to me as a reward for crying."

"You mean your mommy *wants* you to cry?"

"I guess so. Whenever I cry she gives me a lollipop."

"Gee, I'd cry a *lot* more often if I always got a sucker."

"Of course. It's elementary psychology!"

Most people who have seen this sequence just *know* there was something wrong with the way the mother went about trying to reduce crying behavior, although they are often unable to put their finger on exactly what went awry. The sequence makes it seem obvious that crying behavior is not reduced by following it with a lollipop. But why not? Though the sequence doesn't tell us any of the details, it certainly does suggest that there are more successful and less successful ways of interacting with others, more successful and less successful way of influencing others.

What influences are at work in instruction to develop approach or avoidance tendencies? How do the subjects people study in school become objects, activities, and situations that they seek out or avoid?

All the answers to these questions are not yet available, of course, but some things *are* known. If applied, they can increase the instructor's success at causing the things he teaches to be objects and activities of approach rather than of avoidance. Success cannot be guaranteed in all cases, simply because the instructor does not control all of the variables of influence. His best efforts can be neutralized by forces more powerful than those under his control. It is nonetheless true that the instructor can be more successful when he applies what is known about human behavior than when he does not.

A person's native abilities influence the kinds of activities he will engage in and the kinds of objects and events he will tend to approach. But though he may be partial toward those activities at which he is particularly adept, tendencies are influenced primarily by events in the world around him. They are shaped mostly by the attitudes of the people he encounters, by objects and experiences, and by the consequences of his own actions.

People spend a great deal of their time trying to influence other people. They exhort, argue, explain, cajole, and beguile, mostly in an attempt to influence the behavior of another. Sometimes they are successful, sometimes not. Sometimes they are successful when they least desire it; hence, the expression, "Don't do as I do, do as I say."

People are influenced by printed matter and by motion pictures and television. They are influenced to laugh, to cry, to become angry, and to become bored. They are influenced to make a face and back away when they smell a nasty odor; they are influenced to behave otherwise when they smell a delicate perfume or a sizzling steak.

To help you recall some of the events in your own student period that had some influence on the things you now approach or avoid, I will briefly describe a study an associate and I performed not too long ago. This study was designed to chart the history of some tendencies toward academic subjects of 65 ex-students during a half-hour interview.

The first questions of the interview were designed to identify the most favored and the least favored academic subject of each person. Once these subjects were identified, each person was asked a series of questions to determine just how these inclinations got to be that way. These questions were designed to explore each person's feelings about his most-preferred and least-preferred subjects, and to determine what he remembered as the conditions leading to those feelings and to changes in those feelings.

The results of the study were interesting and somewhat unexpected. Almost every person was able to identify the subjects or school activities that were at the top and at the bottom of his "popularity scale." What was unexpected was the responses to the questions attempting to discover why and how these subjects came to be rated as they were.

With regard to *favorite* academic subject, the interviewees seemed able to discuss the subject with some facility; that is, they talked as though they remembered something of the subject. But they seemed to have no clear idea of how it got to be their favorite subject. Though they always had an answer to the question "How did it get to be that way?" it was clear that their answers reflected only vague memories. "Oh, I always liked history," they would say, or "I was born with an interest in art."

When asked about the subject they liked least, the story was different. They seemed to remember little about the subject itself and would often come right out and say, "I don't remember

a thing about _____, and the less I hear of it the better." But they *always* remembered just how they learned to dislike the subject . . . at least they *said* they remembered. They
were quite capable of pinpointing the events or conditions that
they felt were behind their desire to avoid the subject whenever
they could.

We were perfectly aware that some of the interviewees had
faulty memories. What we were looking for, however, were the
conditions and consequences they remembered as having an
effect, whether or not they were correct, so we would know
what they *said* to other people about the subjects they came to
like and dislike.

As you read the sampling of interview summaries that follows, dip back into your own academic history to see if you can
add other conditions and consequences that may influence
approach and avoidance responses toward subjects taught in
school.

Case 1

Favorite subject:	Music.
How it got that way:	I've always liked music. It was just a personal liking. No events had anything to do with it.
Least-favored subject:	English.
How it got that way:	None of the teachers could get down to a level where the students could understand what they were trying to get across. They didn't know how to make the subject interesting.

Case 2

Favorite subject:	Art, in high school; psychology, in college.
How it got that way:	I've always liked art. Mother encouraged art by providing lots of materials. In high school the instructor was very good. Had a good sense of

humor, and worked *with* students. He encouraged us to participate in contests. I still use my art knowledge in my work.

Least-favored subject: Mathematics.

How it got that way: I was skipped to third grade after completing only half of second grade. I missed considerable background and felt lost. The third grade teacher was very impatient and did not believe in individual instruction. She ridiculed me in front of the class. I was above average in all other subjects, but I failed in accounting in college.

Case 3

Favorite subject: History.

How it got that way: I hated math, wasn't good in English, and so, drifted into history. History interest continued through high school, which is as far as I went. I can't remember anything else that influenced my interest in history, but to this day I continue to study the subject as a hobby.

Least-favored subject: Mathematics.

How it got that way: I never could add 2 and 2, and still can't. I changed schools 18 times between first grade and the end of high school. Every time I got to a school, they were studying something for which I had no background, or they were learning something I already knew. Also, there was a grade school teacher who embarrassed me to death. The instructor once caught me counting on my fingers and took me up to the front of the class to make an example of me. It was humiliating.

Case 4

Favorite subject:	Spanish.
How it got that way:	High school instructor was tremendous; she spoke Spanish from the first day and taught class to sing Spanish songs. She encouraged special projects and allowed better students to help slower ones.
Least-favored subject:	None. (No strong avoidance tendencies toward any subject. In college, this person majored in science. There were two reasons for this: (1) A cousin was taking science and interested the student by talking about it enthusiastically and by showing homework and experiments. (2) Student had a high school physiology teacher who had well-organized lectures and a good lab. This instructor checked lab work frequently and showed relevant films that were highly interesting. This instructor was a person to whom students felt they could go with problems. This is an instance where the attitude toward a subject changed over a period of time as the result of events and consequences.)

Case 5

Favorite subject:	Psychology.
How it got that way:	I had a great admiration for the instructor, and felt the course was well

presented. He did not become angry when students disagreed with him ... he was willing to be criticized. He did not ridicule. He encouraged his students and had no discipline problems.

Least-favored subject: Physics.

How it got that way: I felt I didn't have the mind for it. Also, I had a high school instructor I liked, but he merely read the textbook to the class and then assigned problems without giving the necessary information that would help in solving them. This instructor couldn't make himself understood.

To summarize the results of the study, we can say that a favorite subject tends to get that way because the person seems to do well at it, because the subject was associated with liked or admired friends, relatives, or instructors, and because the person was relatively comfortable when in the presence of the subject or activity. A subject least favored tends to get that way because the person seems to have little or no aptitude for it, because the subject is associated with disliked individuals, and because being in the presence of the subject is often associated with unpleasant conditions.

What do you believe to be the conditions and consequences that influenced your behavior toward the subjects you studied in school?

There is no question that nonschool influences may also have had a part in shaping the direction and strength of tendencies expressed by the interviewees in the study. People influence people whether they are teachers, parents, teen-agers, or relatives. Our concern, remember, is not with whether teachers are the *sole* source of influence, but with whether teachers are a *positive* source of influence.

Sources of influence on subject matter tendencies, then, include:

- The **conditions** that surround a subject.
- The **consequences** of coming into contact with a subject.
- The way that others react toward a subject **(modeling).**

Now that some of the sources of influence have been identified, the next task is to find out just how these sources operate and how they may be arranged in order to achieve a desired result.

Exhortation is used more and accomplishes less than almost any behavior-changing tool known to man.

6

Conditions and Consequences

The three ways in which behavior toward objects and events are influenced, which, for our purposes, are referred to as conditions, consequences, and modeling, are not the only ways in which behavior is influenced. They are, however, particularly relevant because they are things we can do something about.

First, Consider Conditions

When the student is in the presence of subject matter,* he should at the same time be in the presence of *positive conditions*. Conversely, when the student is in the presence of subject matter, he should not at the same time be in the presence of *aversive conditions*.**

---

*The term "subject matter" is intended here in its broader sense, not as the mere transmission of facts. It refers to whatever it is you are intending to achieve in the way of educational intents, whether this be knowledge, problem-solving skill, creativity, or motor skills.

**An aversive condition is an event that causes physical or mental discomfort. It is an event that people will try (work) to avoid. Just what these events are will be considered in some detail in Chapter 7.

These two statements infer one way in which objects or events initially neutral can eventually come to evoke approach or avoidance responses. That is, if a subject that initially has no special significance is presented to someone on several occasions while he is experiencing an aversive (unpleasant) condition, that subject may become a signal that triggers an avoidance response. Similarly, if a person is presented with a neutral subject and at the same time is in the presence of positive (pleasant) conditions, that subject may become a signal for an approach response.

Let's examine some everyday examples.

How do you react when a physician moves a hypodermic needle toward your arm? If you are like many people, you tend to back away; if you don't back away physically, you may turn your head to avoid seeing this signal for a forthcoming prick of pain. There is nothing aversive about the sight of the hypodermic needle—the first time you see one, that is. It is a neutral subject. But after you have experienced aversive conditions (pain) while in the presence of a hypodermic needle, it becomes a signal for an avoidance response. It is as though the mere sight of a hypodermic needle becomes a condition to be avoided.

I know a school where to say "Let's go to the boiler room" immediately generates approach responses on the part of the teachers. They go to the boiler room whenever they can, and think kind thoughts about boiler rooms. Why? In *their* school, the boiler room is the faculty lounge; it is the place where pleasant or desirable conditions exist. It is where teachers can relax, talk with their colleagues, and have a smoke. For you, the words "boiler room" don't signal approach or avoidance responses... unless it has been the scene of positive or aversive conditions.

I came across this magnificent example in a letter that recently appeared in Ann Landers' column:

... When my mother took me shopping, I soon learned not to express an opinion. My taste was "atrocious." Hers was "elegant." Once when I saw a dress I really wanted, my mother said, in the presence of the saleswoman, "You are as fat as a pig and that dress makes you look like a freak."

From then on I flatly refused to shop for clothes. I told my mother to bring home whatever she liked and I would wear it. I am a grown woman now, but these horrible memories are as vivid as if they had happened yesterday.

I hate clothes and I wear my dresses till they fall apart. *To this day, I cannot pass the dress section where we used to shop without being physically ill* [italics added].*

Yes, neutral subjects often turn into those that will attract or repel, and you will find many examples of them if you look around. You may not find many that result in the extreme reaction cited in the last example, but they are there nonetheless.

Going back to the study described earlier, there were several instances where the interviewees responded like this:

At first I didn't care much about the subject one way or the other. But the instructor made me feel very comfortable and I began to worry less about a grade and found myself studying the subject more intently than I had planned.

We see, then, that one way of insuring that we are not the cause of an avoidance tendency toward the subject matter we teach is to arrange our instructional system so that when the student is in the presence of the subject matter, he is, at the same time, (1) in the presence of positive conditions and (2) in the presence of as few aversive conditions as possible.

Does this mean that instructional situations should be made "fun" and that the student should not be required to work hard?

Absolutely not! What is suggested is that *under the appropriate conditions students will want to work longer and harder.* This point is too important to gloss over. Consider this dialogue:

"What kind of work do you do?"
"I'm in the sex business."
"The *what?*"
"The sex business. I teach actresses how to kiss."
"And you call that *work?*"
"—It's a living."

*"Ann Landers," reprinted by permission of San Jose *Mercury* and Publishers-Hall Syndicate.

This may seem an unlikely conversation, but it does serve to illustrate some of the confusion surrounding the word "work." This word has come to have several meanings. Sometimes it is used to refer to an occupation or profession, as in "What kind of work do you do?" When used this way, it seldom carries with it connotations of good or bad, pleasant or unpleasant. But *work* is also often used to refer to an activity that one would prefer to avoid, as in "Oh, that's work," or "I'd rather be enjoying myself, but I've got work to do." In these cases, the implication is that the activity referred to is one the speaker finds distasteful.

There is another way in which *work* is given a bad name. The familiar expression, "All work and no play makes Jack a dull boy," clearly implies that *play* is fun and *work* is not. What a horrible fate for a perfectly respectable word.

Were you to check your dictionary, you would find that *work* is "the expenditure of energy directed toward the accomplishment of something." It is engaging in some sort of purposeful activity. Skiing is work, swimming is work, playing the banjo is work, and so is writing. Haven't you ever engaged in purposeful activity that was exciting, engrossing, exhilarating, or just plain enjoyable? Haven't you ever heard anyone say, "I like my work?" Don't you like your work?

There must be something other than the expenditure of energy that causes the word "work" to have an aversive connotation with some activities and not with others. That something is the *conditions* associated with the activity, or the *consequences* following the activity.

> When energy expenditure is associated with aversive conditions, that activity will tend to become aversive; when the energy expenditure is followed regularly by aversive consequences (punishment), that activity will tend to be avoided.

I can see absolutely nothing wrong with making students work. There is nothing wrong with making them work hard. But there are an infinite number of ways in which you can arrange the situation, *there are a lot of things you can do to them while they are working* . . . while they are in the presence of your favorite academic activity.

By all means make assignments, and by all means expect them to be carried out, on time. But also do your best to see that these activities are associated with positive conditions and with as few aversive conditions as possible. After all, even under the best of circumstances you will not cause everyone to be wild about your favorite subject. But professional practice demands that you do everything in your power to make certain you don't accidentally destroy whatever interest is already there. *Don't confuse work with unpleasantness.*

Now, We'll Explore Consequences

Whenever contact with subject matter is followed by *positive consequences,* the subject will tend to become a stimulus for approach responses. Conversely, whenever contact with subject matter is followed by *aversive consequences,* the subject may become a stimulus for avoidance responses.

Imagine yourself a student again. When you correctly answer a question posed by your instructor, the instructor smiles and says something like "Good." When you answer his question incorrectly, he makes a comment such as, "Well, let's look at the question again." Wouldn't the probability increase that you will be willing to answer questions and come into contact with the subject matter? In any case, this kind of interaction would not adversely influence your responses toward the subject. Conversely, suppose each time you answer a question the instructor says, "Well I see old Dumbo is at it again." How long do you think it would be before you stopped raising your hand? How long do you think it would be before you began to think of excuses for not attending class?

When experience with a subject is *followed* by a positive (pleasant) consequence, the probability is increased that the subject will be approached again in the future. (Think for a moment about one or two people you like and ask yourself what there is about them that makes you want to be with them.)

When, on the other hand, experience with a subject is followed by aversive (unpleasant) consequences, the probability is reduced that the subject will be approached in the future.

> If you want to increase the probability that a response will be repeated, follow it immediately by a positive consequence. If you want to reduce the probability that the behavior will occur again, follow it immediately by an aversive consequence.

To see whether I have explained this principle in a satisfactory manner, answer the question that follows this example of human interaction.

> *Secretary:*   Here's the report you wanted, boss. I worked all week end so that I could give it to you before you caught your plane.
>
> *Boss:*   Good grief, Mary, haven't you learned how to spell "achieve" yet?

Do you think that Mary will be more likely or less likely to spend her week ends getting something done for her boss?

More likely.............................*Turn to page 45.*
Less likely..............................*Turn to page 46.*

More likely?

Hmm. The secretaries of your acquaintance must get their kicks in rather strange ways if their world becomes brighter when they are chastised for their spelling. If such a comment is taken as a *compliment* though, your choice of answer is all right. But honestly, don't you think most hard-working girls would be more than a little crushed if their efforts were followed by such a consequence?

Return to page 44 and look at the interaction again.

Less likely?

Yes. When the result of an action is that something unpleasant or undesirable happens, the chance that that action will be repeated is reduced. People simply do not often deliberately do things that will bring on aversive consequences.

If you know someone who seems to be an exception, ask yourself this magic question: What event or condition is maintaining, or rewarding, the behavior in question? If you look closely, you will find that the aversive consequence associated with the behavior is being overshadowed by a positive consequence of somewhat greater value (strength). For example, if you examine why a child *continues* to engage in some behavior even though a parent always runs over and yells "Stop that!" you will likely find that the reward value of the *attention* received from the admonition is stronger than the punishment value of the threat.

Let's look at one more example:

> *Wife:*   Not now . . . I've got to do the dishes.
> *Husband:*   All right, Honey. I'll help you.

Does it look as though the frequency of the wife's procrastinations will increase or decrease as a result of the husband's reaction?

Increase...*Turn to page 48.*
Decrease.......................................*Turn to page 47.*

Decrease? Hardly.

Perhaps you erred here because I failed to mention an important aspect of the consequences principle, that for an action to be less likely to occur the consequence must be aversive *to the one performing the action*. The same is true for positive consequences. It doesn't matter what *I* might seek out or avoid; it is what is positive or aversive to the person whose behavior I am trying to influence that counts. And this, incidentally, is one reason we don't succeed more often than we do in the area of human interaction. We try to influence others by providing consequences that are positive to us but not to them.

When you try to influence someone's actions by giving him what he "ought" to want instead of what he *does* want . . . well, good luck.

Remember the consequences principle: When an action leads to an undesirable consequence, that action is *less* likely to occur again in the future. When an action leads to a desirable consequence, the action is *more* likely to be repeated.

Take another look at the example on page 46. Then select the other answer.

Increase? You bet!

When an action is followed by a positive (pleasant) consequence—when an action leads to a desired outcome—the likelihood that it will be repeated is increased.

Whenever you want to analyze the effect of an interaction (an action followed by a reaction or consequence), ask yourself whether the consequence is positive or aversive to the person *performing the action*. If the consequence is positive to the one performing the action, the likelihood of the action being repeated is increased; if the consequence is aversive to the one performing the action, the likelihood of the action being repeated is decreased.

> **To increase the likelihood of a student's coming into contact with your favorite subject, accentuate the positive conditions and consequences and eliminate the negative, the aversive.**

People learn to avoid the things
they are hit with.

7

Positives and Aversives

To help you apply the conditions and consequences principles more effectively, we'll examine positive and aversive events
in more detail. Although it isn't always possible to know
whether an event is positive or aversive for a given individual,
some conditions and consequences are universal enough in their
effect to provide considerable guidance. So that we can end this
chapter on a positive note, let's consider conditions and consequences that are aversive first.

> An **aversive condition or consequence** is any event
> that causes physical or mental discomfort. It is any
> event that causes a person to think less highly of him-
> self, that leads to a loss of self-respect or dignity, or
> that results in a strong anticipation of any of these. In
> general, any condition or consequence may be con-
> sidered aversive if it causes a person to feel smaller or
> makes his world dimmer.

There are several conditions and consequences that are avoided by enough people to warrant their being referred to as *universal aversives*. When these conditions or consequences are associated with the subjects we teach or appear as a result of subject matter contact, then the subject matter, learning, or even school itself may take on a less desirable hue . . . and no amount of righteous indignation on our part will alter this effect, no declaiming of how the student "ought" to be more interested will have nearly as much effect toward that end as reducing the aversive characteristics of the learning situation.

On the pages that follow, some universal aversives will be described and illustrated with examples of school practices.

Pain

is an acute physical discomfort, as you very well know. Though there are probably no longer many teacher-provoked occasions where a student is in pain when in the presence of subject matter or as a consequence of approaching subject matter, the event is by no means unheard of.

I know a violin instructor who, in an angry attempt to get his student's fingers properly positioned, makes those fingers hurt. He makes his students cry with pain and tremble with fear. His claim that this is "good" for his student is nothing more than justification for his uncommon version of educational malpractice.

Perhaps the only remaining instance of the pain universal aversive in schools, though almost extinct, is that of hitting a student as a response to something he has or has not done. Understand that the concern here is not with whether punishment should or should not be allowed, but with the effects of conditions and consequences on the subject matter approach behavior of the student. In this case, if the student is to be bashed because of something he has done or not done, see to it that the bashing is done someplace where the student is not in the presence of the subject matter, and see to it that the bashing is done with something *other than* the subject matter.

There are instances of the pain universal aversive that do not directly involve the instructor or school. Sometimes, for example, a student is in pain when he is trying to read; if a student has an uncorrected eye condition, trying to read can actually hurt.

Fear and anxiety

are distress or uneasiness of the mind: apprehension of danger, misfortune, or pain; tension, foreboding, worry, or disquiet; anticipation of the unpleasant.

Procedures leading to fear and anxiety are those that threaten various forms of unpleasantness. They include:

- Telling the student by word or deed that nothing he can do will lead to success, or that contact with the subject will lead to undesirable consequences.

- Telling the student, "You won't understand this, but . . . ."

- Telling the student, "It ought to be perfectly obvious that . . . ."

- Threatening the exposure of "ignorance" by forcing the student to solve problems at the chalkboard in front of the class.

- Basing an attrition rate on administrative fiat rather than on student performance ("Half of you won't be here a month from now," or "I don't believe in giving high grades").

- Threatening failure by telling the student, "If you aren't motivated enough, you shouldn't be here." (*Translation:* "If you aren't motivated enough to learn in spite of my poor teaching, you certainly aren't going to get any help from me.")

- Being unpredictable about the standard of acceptable performance. (For example, a sixth grade teacher recently told his students that they didn't have to listen to his discussion if they were having no difficulty with its topic. Five minutes later he berated half the class for "not paying attention.")

- A common form of punishment in some schools is "going to see the principal." Because of some real or imagined infraction, the student is sent to the principal's office, where vengeance is expected to be wreaked upon the student by the principal. How many times have I seen a poor young student sitting there waiting for the verbal lash—small, frightened, and bewildered—starting in fright at the smallest movement. *This is education?*

Frustration

is a condition or consequence that occurs when goal-directed activities are blocked, when purposeful or motivated activity is interfered with. To frustrate is to thwart, to foil, to circumvent, to interfere with, to check, to make an effort come to no avail, to nullify, to defeat. Practices that can generate frustration include:

- Presenting information in larger units, or at a faster pace, than the student can assimilate. (The more motivated the student is, the greater the frustration when his efforts are blocked.) Jack Vaughn describes this as the situation where the student came to drink from the fountain of knowledge and somebody turned on a fire hose.

- Speaking too softly to be heard easily (blocking the student's effort to come into contact with the subject).

- Keeping secret the intent of the instruction, or the way in which performance will be evaluated.

- Providing unreadable print; type too small or too ornate, reading level too high.

- Providing obscure text, or implying more profundity than actually exists, as in, "When two parallel lines are cut by a transversal, the alternate interior angles are equal."

- Teaching one set of skills, and then testing for another.

- Testing for skills other than those stated in announced objectives.

- Refusing to answer student questions.

- Using test items with obscure meanings.
- Forcing all students to proceed at the same pace, thus frustrating the slow and boring the quick.
- Calling a halt when a student is absorbed with his instruction or attempting to complete a project (ringing a school bell, for example).
- When a well-meaning teacher trying to get his material across doesn't set up adequate feedback or consequences, or if the consequences are so remote in time that the student doesn't associate them with the learning activity, a frustration situation exists. The student is trying to do well, but his efforts simply go unrecognized (for example, delaying the return of test results).

Humiliation and embarrassment

are caused by lowering a person's pride or self-respect, by making him uncomfortably self-conscious; by shaming, debasing, or degrading him; or by causing him a painful loss of dignity. Procedures that lead to these conditions include:

- Publicly comparing a student unfavorably with others.
- Laughing at a student's efforts. When Dr. David Cram returned his comments on the original draft of this book, he included the following:

  My own pappy relates his music career thusly: "We had a singing session and the teacher asked me to sing alone. When I did, all the kids laughed. The next day he asked me to do it again. Well, sir, I wouldn't do it. So the teacher made me come to the front of the class, but I still wouldn't do it. So he hit my hand with a ruler. But he could have cut off my fingers and I *still* wouldn't have done it. I didn't, either. Ever!"

- Spotlighting a student's weaknesses by bringing them to the attention of the class.
- Making a student wear a badge of his "stupidity" (putting him in a special seat or section, for example).
- Belittling a student's attempt to approach the subject by such replies to his questions as "Stop trying to show off."

- Insulting a student for his attempt to approach the subject by such comments as, "You couldn't possibly understand the answer to that question," or otherwise telling him by word or deed that his questions are considered stupid.

- Repeated failure. It is perfectly appropriate to challenge students enough to cause them to fail on occasion, provided that the consequence of failure is not an avoidable aversive situation. Repeated failure, however, is sure to lead a student to think less highly of himself and to try to avoid the situation that has come to signify such a shrinkage of self-esteem. Repeated failure is often engineered into our educational system. One practice is that of grading on a curve. Whenever performance is evaluated by comparing it with what a group of chance neighbors happens to do, a person with the below-average aptitude will almost always come out on the lower half of the curve. He may have achieved all the objectives set out for him; he may have learned to work faster or more effectively; he may be exceeding the standard set out by the instructor. No matter. When his performance is compared with that of more talented neighbors, he will always be the loser. This use of the curve is only slightly less reprehensible than the instructor who brags that he has a "tough" course because 40 per cent of his class "failed." (Has it ever occurred to him that he is only 60 per cent successful?)

- The "special class" set up for students the teacher is not competent enough to cope with. Students are singled out and sent to another place for a variety of remedial treatment. They are branded as "different" and somehow inadequate. (In one state, first and second graders with minor speech deficiencies are sent to a special class and taught that they are *handicapped* persons. They are taught stories about Helen Keller and others who have had severe handicaps. They are taught that they, too, must overcome their special "burden" if they are to succeed. Such a practice can only be labeled "Crimes We Commit in the Name of Education.")

- A common elementary school practice leading to humiliation and embarrassment frequently occurs after a teacher has asked the class a question. In almost every class there seems to be at least one student who is so anxious to come into contact with the subject, so eager to demonstrate his competence, that while frantically waving his hand in the air the answer slips out from between his lips. What is the consequence of this behavior on the part of the student? Does his world become a little brighter, is he encouraged to think more highly of himself as a result of his action? Sometimes. Often, however, the consequence is a finger pointed sternly in his direction followed by, "I . . . didn't . . . call . . . on . . . you!" And what the student is learning is that it doesn't pay to get very excited about the things that happen in school, that showing too much interest can have unpleasant results, that showing excitement can lead to embarrassment, to humiliation. Oh, I know. Students must be taught discipline (and discipline *will* be a problem as long as students are forced to sit in neat little rows listening to lectures). But there are better ways of handling discipline problems, ways that do not embarrass the student while in the presence of the subject matter.

Boredom

is caused by a situation in which the stimuli impinging on the student are weak, repetitive, or infrequent. Typical avoidance responses are those of leaving the situation and of falling asleep. Procedures leading to boredom include:

- Presenting information in a monotone.
- Rocking rhythmically back and forth while speaking.
- Insisting the student sit through instruction covering something that he already knows.
- Using impersonal, passive language.
- Providing information in increments so small that they provide no challenge or require no effort.
- Allowing lethargy-inducing temperatures to exist.

- Using only a single mode of presentation (no variety).
- Reading the textbook aloud. Consider for a moment the effect on a student of the instructor whose principal technique is to read aloud from the textbook. If a student has prepared himself for the class by studying the assignment in the textbook, he is punished for his effort in the classroom through the boredom of repetition. How can the student avoid some of the boredom of this situation? Very simply. He can stop doing his textbook assignments before coming to class. In this way, although he may suffer through a dull reading of the textbook during the class hour, at least the material read will not be familiar. This is one situation where the student is rewarded for being less, rather than more, diligent. He is reinforced for disregarding the assignments of his instructor. Since this situation is one in which the student's act of entering the classroom is followed by an unpleasant event (boredom), and since people tend to avoid unpleasant events, the student will simply try to avoid attending class whenever possible. And why not? Are *you* eager to place yourself in a boring situation? (Wake up there!)

Physical discomfort
is an uneasiness, a hardship, mild pain. Though there are several ways of inducing physical discomfort while the student is in the presence of a subject, most of them are not under the direct control of the instructor. A partial list would include:

- Allowing excessive noise or other distractions.
- Insisting the student be physically passive for longer periods of time than his state of development can tolerate. (Here is an example of how discomfort, combined with a reward, led to a most unexpected result. A woman had a ten-year-old son who attended Sunday school with some reluctance. She wanted him to feel more positively toward church. The technique she selected for achieving this goal

was to make the boy attend the *regular* service that followed the Sunday school session. The boy found the regular service a very uncomfortable affair indeed. He had to sit in a hard pew . . . he had to be quiet . . . he had to restrain himself from fidgeting. In addition, he was expected to listen to something he didn't understand at all. Since "sitting in church" was aversive, it was rewarding to leave church, because church-leaving led to a turning off of the discomfort. Result: Church became a symbol of discomfort and boredom, and was avoided whenever possible.)

- Insisting that the student pay close attention immediately after a meal.

- Making the student travel farther between classrooms than can easily be accomplished in the time allotted.

- Making the classroom too hot or too cold.

One school practice that produces aversive conditions and consequences appears to be so common that I want to comment on it separately. This is the practice of using subject matter as an instrument of punishment. You know how it goes: "All right, because you were unruly you can just stay after school and work twenty-five arithmetic problems"; or "For that you can just read four chapters tonight instead of the one chapter I was going to assign." Again, the issue has nothing to do with the appropriateness or inappropriateness of punishment. It concerns only the *instrument* of punishment. People tend to avoid the things they are hit with, whether it be a club, a stick, or a subject matter assignment.

You might think, after reading the section on universal aversives, that I regard school as nothing but a big bag of aversive conditions and that I think teachers do little else than dispense aversive consequences. Nothing could be further from the truth. Although there is no shortage of aversive conditions and consequences, the balance is in favor of the positive. It's just that the aversives are so easy to spot; they stand out like blackbirds in a cherry pie.

A **positive condition or consequence** is any pleasant event that exists during the time the student is in the presence of the subject matter, or that follows his approach to the subject matter. In the way that an aversive condition or consequence causes the student's world to become dimmer or causes him to think less highly of himself, a positive condition or consequence causes the student to think a little more highly of himself, causes his world to become a little brighter.

Conditions and consequences that are *universal positives* are just the opposite of the universal aversives. They are the events that lead to success experiences and acknowledge that success, insure a variety of stimulation, lead to an increase of self-esteem or improved self-image, and lead to an increase in confidence. Positive practices include:

- Acknowledging students' responses, whether correct or incorrect, as attempts to learn, and following them with accepting rather than rejecting comments ("No, you'll have to try again," rather than "How could you make such a stupid error!").
- Reinforcing or rewarding subject approach responses.
- Providing instruction in increments that will allow success most of the time.
- Eliciting learning responses in private rather than in public.
- Providing enough signposts so that the student always knows where he is and where he is expected to go.
- Providing the student with statements of your instructional objectives that *he* can understand when he first sees them.
- Detecting what the student already knows and dropping that from his curriculum (thus not boring him by teaching him what he already knows).
- Providing feedback that is immediate and specific to the student's response.

- Giving the student some choice in selecting and sequencing subject matter (especially where you maintain rigid control over the goals of the instruction), thus making positive involvement possible.
- Providing the student with some control over the length of the instructional session.
- Relating new information to old, within the experience of the student.
- Treating the student as a person rather than as a number in a faceless mass.
- Using active rather than passive words during presentations.
- Making use of those variables known to be successful in attracting and holding human attention, such as motion, color, contrast, variety, and personal reference.
- For administrators only: Allowing only those instructors who like and are enthusiastic about their subjects (and students) to teach.
- Making sure the student can perform with ease, not just barely, so that confidence can be developed.
- Expressing genuine delight at seeing the student (*Delighted* to see you again!).
- Expressing genuine delight at seeing the student succeed.
- Providing instructional tasks that are relevant to your objectives.
- Using only those test items relevant to your objectives.
- Allowing students to move about as freely as their physiology and their curiosity demand.

Going back to the study described in Chapter 5 again, here are some of the comments interviewees made about teacher practices they believed to have a positive influence on their interest in the subject under discussion:

He taught us how to approach a problem so we could solve it for ourselves. He gave us the tools for learning.

He broke the subject matter down into pieces we could understand. When we couldn't understand something, he tried to find another way of approaching it.

He made books available at our level. That is, these were books that answered questions we had about the subject at that particular time.

The instructor reinforced our desire to learn by giving us assistance and by showing a personal interest in what we were doing.

He led discussions, but did not dominate them.

He had a magnificent manner of presentation; he taught history as though it were a news analysis course, tying current happenings to historical happenings.

He was always able to make the student understand what was expected of him and where he stood.

She used a lot of variety; she brought in other instructors, used films and demonstrations rather than pure lecture.

He asked, and respected, the opinion of students . . . even though he didn't always agree with them.

He knew his subject and always appeared to have time.

There is nothing revolutionary about the procedures listed in this chapter. Every instructor who is interested in increasing the capabilities of his students uses many or all of them, and quite a few others as well.

Then why go into such detail? Simple because *good intentions are not enough.* Though we are generally in favor of sending students away at least as interested in our subject as they were when they arrived, we do little or nothing to *insure* that this is the case. Such apathy is frightening if one considers that the continuing use of factors leading to subject avoidance represents an enormous loss of potential skills. Those lost skills may well be one of the greatest burdens our economy will have to carry as we move into an age where a man without skills is virtually unemployable.

8

Modeling

It has not been my intention to suggest that the only ways in which behavior is influenced are by the conditions associated with subject matter approach and the consequences following subject matter contact. The stress has been on these aspects because it is here that the large improvement can be made with little effort and with little or no cost.

Another way in which behavior is strongly influenced is that of modeling, or *learning by imitation*. "Don't do as I do, do as I say," is a recognition of the fact that people sometimes learn more from imitation than we would like. A little girl doesn't dress up in her mother's clothes and high heels because she has been taught to do so; she is doing as she has seen her mother do. Frequently, a little boy imitates his father's automobile driving behavior (sometimes including the unsavory comments he has heard, possibly thinking it is a necessary part of the driving ritual).

It is by modeling that we learn how to behave in most unfamiliar situations. Suppose you suddenly had to attend a White House tea, and that you had never had an opportunity to enter that establishment before. How would you know how to behave? Very likely, you would watch to see what others did and then do likewise; you would use others as a model of what is expected or appropriate. To paraphrase Dr. Albert Bandura, if it weren't for the fact that we learn a great deal by imitation, there probably wouldn't be as many of us as there are; if we had to learn everything through trial and error, or by making responses and then having them corrected, a lot fewer of us would survive.*

Dr. Bandura has been experimenting with the effects of modeling for many years. "In our research at Stanford University," he says, "we have found that almost any learning outcome that results from direct experience can also come about on a vicarious basis through observation of other people's behavior and its consequences for them."**

One of the thought-provoking experiments performed by this pioneer in behavior change had to do with children's behavior toward an ordinary Bobo doll. Nursery school children watched adults perform in different ways toward the doll. One group watched an adult hitting and saying aggressive things to the doll, another group watched adults behave more kindly toward the doll, and a third group didn't see any modeling cues at all. Even though these young children had no opportunity to *practice* or *rehearse* what they had seen, ". . . children who had observed the aggressive models displayed a large number of precisely matching aggressive responses, whereas such patterns of behavior rarely occurred in either the nonaggressive-model

*Albert Bandura, "Vicarious Processes: A Case of No-trial Learning," in *Advances in Experimental Social Psychology, Vol. 2.* New York: Academic Press, Inc., 1965, pp. 1-55.

**Albert Bandura, "Behavioral Psychotherapy," *Scientific American,* No. 216 (1967), pp. 78-86.

condition or the control group."* In other words, the children tended to act toward the doll in the same way they saw the adult acting. Those who watched an adult who hit the doll *also* tended to hit the doll. Those who did not watch an adult hit the doll rarely acted in such an aggressive way themselves.

Among the conclusions that can be reached from Dr. Bandura's modeling experiments are these:

1. Students learn more by imitation if the model has prestige (for the student).
2. The student will *perform* more of what he has learned if he has seen the model being reinforced rather than punished for that performance.
3. When a student sees a model being punished, the student will tend not to engage in the kind of behavior that was punished.
4. When a student sees a model doing things he shouldn't do (transgressions) and there is no aversive consequence to the model, there is an increase in the probability that the student will do those undesirable things.

The research on modeling tells us that *if we would maximize subject matter approach tendencies in our students we must exhibit those behaviors ourselves.* In other words, we must behave the way we want our students to behave.

Although a display of interest and enthusiasm is not enough to guarantee that the student will come to display similar feelings, the probability is certainly greater that this will happen than if we display apathy and disinterest. Conversely, a display of apathy on our part doesn't prevent a student from becoming more interested in our topics . . . but it doesn't help. Recent research has confirmed the fact that when you teach one thing and model something else, the teaching is less effective than if you practice what you teach.** The father, for example, whose

*"Albert Bandura, "Social Learning Through Imitation," in M. R. Jones (ed.), *Nebraska Symposium on Motivation: 1962*, Lincoln, Nebr.: University of Nebraska Press, 1962, pp. 211-269.

**David Rosenhan, Frank Frederick, and Anne Burrowes, "Preaching and Practicing: Effects of Channel Discrepancy on Norm Internalization, *Child Development*, Vol. 39, No. 1 (March, 1968), pp. 291-301.

approach is to say, "Stop fighting with the other kids or I'll whip you good," is less likely to be successful than if he were to model the kind of behavior he is interested in teaching. Parents are less likely to teach their kids to love their neighbor when the parents continually fight among themselves than if they were to model the behavior they want to teach. And, as Dr. Bandura suggests, the father who exhorts his children to work hard in school, while he guzzles beer in front of the TV, is less likely to see the desired behavior than if he were to model the beaver instead of the sloth.

What students learn by imitation, however, is not confined to their attitudes relating to various academic topics. For example, one professor who teaches psychology spends a great deal of time teaching students how to read and interpret journal articles. He teaches them how to recognize the difference between data and the interpretation of data, and how to recognize the difference between adequate and inadequate controls. While doing this, he is also modeling a certain kind of behavior with regard to criticism. When a student condemns a research report because of a design flaw, this instructor says, "Perhaps. But what is the author trying to say? What is good about the study?" When a student is hypercritical because of the way in which a report is written, the instructor asks, "How could he have said it better?" In other words, rather than model nit-picking criticism, this instructor models positive criticism, and it is likely his students will learn to do the same. If we would like to increase the frequency with which our students think critically, or open-mindedly, we have a better chance of succeeding if we demonstrate these qualities ourselves. If we would have our students demonstrate a love for learning, we have a better chance of succeeding if we demonstrate that a quest for knowledge is more important than simple parroting of what is in the text.

Are we models worthy of imitation?

We have considered two of the ways in which behavior toward a subject may be influenced: by the conditions associated with subject matter approach and by the consequences of subject matter contact. In addition, some of the effects of modeling have been mentioned.

There are other procedures that are more or less effective in influencing behavior, but a thorough discussion of each is beyond the scope of this book. I will only mention that *exhortation,* a procedure used regularly for centuries, has seldom been very successful in influencing behavior ("Pay close attention now, because in several weeks this material will become very important!"), and that the instructor who does little more than *insist* his students be interested, or *insist* they be motivated, will certainly have cause for complaining about student apathy.

Approach and avoidance behaviors, then, are influenced by the things we do and by the things we say . . . whether we will it or not. To the extent that we come to recognize and apply those practices leading to approach behavior, we will come closer to reaching our objective of sending students away at least as favorably disposed toward our topic as they were when they came to us.

How Will
I Know I've
Arrived?

"You can't measure the effects of what I do."
"Why not?"
"They're intangible."
"Oh? Why should I pay you for intangible results?"
"Because I've been trained and licensed to practice."
"Hmm . . . all right. Here's your money."
"Where? I don't see it."
"Of course not . . . it's intangible."

9

Evaluating Results

Unless we act to evaluate our success in influencing subject matter approach tendencies, we can't substantiate any claims we might make in that direction. More importantly, we won't have as many clues as to how we might improve our efforts.

There are two kinds of evaluation to be considered. One is an assessment of whether our students appear to be as willing to approach our subject at the end of our influence as they were when it began. The other is the assessment of how well we are applying the conditions and consequences principles described in the preceding chapters. In other words, one is the evaluation of *results* and the other is the evaluation of *process*. Results evaluation tells us something about how well we are doing; process evaluation tells us how we might do better.

We'll Begin with Results Evaluation

At first glance, the problem of finding out whether our students are as interested in our subject at the end of the course as they were at the beginning seems insurmountable. If it were not so important, we might be tempted to give up before we began.

One reason the task seems so difficult is that there is not too much experience to draw on; our teaching predecessors were not noted for the zeal with which they developed techniques to *measure* their success in influencing student "attitudes."

The problem, however, looks larger than it really is. After all, we are not concerned with hair-splitting measurements of tendency strengths; we are concerned only with discovering whether tendencies are positive or negative. We have enough work to do to eliminate the negative to worry too much at this point about fine gradations of tendency strengths.

There is another reason why the problem is not as large as it first appears. The results of any evaluation of our success at influencing approach tendencies are for *ourselves,* not for our students. We don't grade students on whether or not they exhibit approach behavior toward our subject ("You get an 'A' in math, but you flunk in attitude"). If any "grading" is to be done, it must be of ourselves. Since the student will seldom see, and never feel, the direct effects of a tendency evaluation, we can be somewhat less concerned about the perfection of our measurement practices.

There is yet another reason why tendency evaluation is a manageable problem: Statements about tendencies are inferences or predictions based upon approach behaviors . . . and approach behaviors are quite tangible.

Since there is something to be learned from earlier attempts to measure so-called intangibles, we will begin there.

For many years, there was a serious search for what might be called the single-measure test of intelligence. Scientists measured the length of the forehead or the number and location of bumps on the head and tried to correlate their measurements with something called *intelligence.* But it was all in vain.

For one thing, there is no such "thing" as intelligence in the sense that there is a heart and a brain. Intelligence is not a structure or an organ that can be measured with a pair of calipers or a scale. Intelligence is a capability or capacity that cannot be accurately predicted by any *single* physical measurement.

The second reason the attempt to find the single-measure test of intelligence failed is that intelligence is a multifaceted characteristic that can only be inferred indirectly. That is to say, intelligence is a characteristic that is inferred from circumstantial evidence. It is a form of prediction about what a person would do, or about how skillfully he might handle a given situation, based on what a person has been seen to do.

The search for the single-measure test of intelligence finally gave way to a search for a *combination* of behavior samples (items) that might give a more realistic prediction about the general and specific nature of the invisible characteristic called intelligence than any single item could do by itself. Today, all tests used to make inferences about intelligence consist of several items . . . all tests used are devices for collecting behavior samples.

The experience with intelligence testing is very similar to that which occurs when we undertake to make statements about the condition of a student's knowledge or understanding. Rather than make such statements on the basis of a single test item, we prefer to make such statements on the basis of responses to several, or many test items. We have more confidence in statements about knowledge and understanding when they are based on the responses to a variety of items than when they are based on a response to a single item.

Similarly, we will have more confidence in statements about approach or avoidance tendencies when these statements are based upon a pattern of responses than when they are based on only a single response. This may be quite an obvious point, but it deserves emphasis because of what is to follow. A variety of items will be presented for your consideration for possible use in assessing your success in achieving your affective objective. Unless you keep in mind that no single item is intended to stand by itself, you might be tempted to reject an item as not providing *all* the information from which suitable inferences can be made.

As you will recall from Chapter 4, there are two kinds of evidence useful as indicators of tendency, things the student *says* and things the student *does*. These can be subdivided into things the student might say or do *in* or *out of* your presence. Although many responses might be used as tendency indicators, we must restrict ourselves to those that are practical and convenient to observe. (The student who whispers in his girlfriend's ear, "Ahhh, *ma cherie*, I love you almost as much as my test tubes," may be indicating a strong approach toward chemistry, but such verbal behavior is hard to come by.)

The question to answer is this: What might students say or do that would lead me to believe that they are favorably, or unfavorably, disposed toward my subject? (What nuggets of behavior would you consider worth putting on the positive or negative pans of the scales of affect?)

As already implied, it isn't practical to follow a student around waiting for him to come into contact with the subject matter so that you may note his response, just as it isn't practical to wait until a student happens to face a problem requiring calculation and then note how good his math skill is. Therefore, the procedure will be to note student response to the subject through a questionnaire (or direct questioning*) and through observation of a number of subject-related behaviors.

*Don't neglect direct questions. Sometimes the direct approach is quickest, least expensive, and most valid. Probably the best way for me to find out whether you like pistachio nuts is to come right out and ask you. If you say, "I like them very much," I have better evidence from which to infer an approach tendency than if I had not asked such a direct question. We can learn a lot about people simply by asking them direct questions.

An experiment was once described to me that bears on the importance of the direct question. The military was reported to have conducted an experiment to find out how they could predict which soldiers would perform well in Arctic weather. They gave a large number of soldiers personality and aptitude tests, they measured blood pressure and other physiological variables, and they used questionnaires. After all the data were gathered, analyzed, and digested, they found that the best prognosticator of whether a man would function well in Arctic weather was simply to ask him "Do you like cold weather?" If the man replied "Heck, no!" it was a sure bet that he wouldn't do well in the Arctic.

Questionnaire Items

Since instructional environments differ in many ways, it is not possible to provide a complete questionnaire that will work in all situations. You will have to consider the items that follow as suggestions. Use the ones that apply, and derive your own from those that don't apply directly. Although the items are numbered consecutively, they are not listed in any order of importance.

1. Do you intend to take another course in___ _ _ _ ?
   a. Yes.
   b. No.
   c. I'm not sure.

2. How interested are you in taking another course in _____?
   a. Very interested.
   b. Somewhat interested.
   c. I don't care one way or the other.
   d. Not too interested.
   e. Not at all interested.

3. How interested are you in learning more about_____?
   a. Very interested.
   b. Somewhat interested.
   c. I don't care one way or the other.
   d. Not too interested.
   e. Not at all interested.

4. If I had it to do all over again, I (would/would not) have taken this course.

5. I find the subject of___ _ _____.
   a. Very interesting.
   b. Somewhat interesting.
   c. Somewhat uninteresting.
   d. Very uninteresting.

6. List all the subjects you are now taking and then rank order them from most interesting to least interesting.

   [*Leave adequate space for the answer.*]

There are items that will bring the student more directly into contact with the subject. Since there may be a difference between what someone says and what he does, such "behavioral choice" items are useful. They come closer to requiring a commitment relating to the topic under discussion.

7. If someone suggested that you take up _____ as your life's work, what would you reply?

   _____

   _____

8. If you were asked to give a short talk about your favorite school subject, which subject would you talk about?

   _____

9. What would you reply if, in a bull session, someone said, "_____ is very, very important, and everybody should try to learn as much about it as possible."

   _____

   _____

10. Write a paragraph about your favorite school subject.

    [*Leave adequate space for the answer.*]

11. Which of the following subjects would you be most interested in teaching?

    [*List your subject and other subjects the student is studying.*]

    a. _____
    b. _____
    c. _____
    d. _____

Another kind of item, generally called the adjective checklist, presents the student with a series of words that might express his feeling and asks him to circle the words that do.

12. Circle each of the words that tell how you feel (mostly) about the subject of _____.

interesting	boring	worthless
dull	useful	cool
fun	useless	square
too hard	too easy	groovy
exciting	very important	up tight

Since it gives the student several quick opportunities to indicate a choice, an item modeled after the paired comparison may also be useful. It is simple to construct: (1) List your subject and three or four other subjects the student might be currently studying; (2) make a list of pairs of these subjects, pairing each subject once with every other subject; (3) reverse the order of some of the pairs so that each subject is listed first about as many times as it is listed second; and (4) mix up the order of the items. With each subject paired at least once with every other subject, the student is asked to consider two subjects at a time and indicate a preference. A somewhat better index of his inclinations is thus gained than if he were to comment on each subject by itself. Instructions to the student may vary; he might be asked which of the two subjects of a pair he likes best, which of the two does he find more interesting, for which of the two would he give up a Saturday afternoon to learn more about, and so on. It is preferable to put each pair of subjects on a separate piece of paper, for later choices might be influenced by the pattern of earlier choices—the student might look back to make sure he is "consistent," for example. (A convenient way of handling this problem is to use narrow slips of paper, stapled on one side, with one pair of subjects on each slip.) Interpretation of this item is easy, since interest is confined to a single subject. For each student, count the number of times your subject has been circled. In the example given below, each student could circle algebra from zero to three times. If there were twenty students in the class, algebra might be chosen from zero to sixty times, and the "score" might therefore range anywhere from zero to sixty. If you administer the questionnaire at the beginning of your course and then during or at the end of your course, you can compare the results. If the second "score" is at least as large as the first, you might legitimately infer that attitude hasn't been seriously impaired.

13. On the slips of paper that follow, you are given pairs of subjects. Look at the pairs one at a time and draw a circle around the subject you personally find the more interesting of the two.

1.	algebra	English
2.	history	science
3.	algebra	history
4.	English	science
5.	science	algebra
6.	history	English

There is another behavioral-choice item you may be willing to use as one basis for predicting future behavior. The student is given pairs of paragraphs, each paragraph headed by the name of a subject and concerning some aspect of that subject. He is asked to pick one of the pair of paragraphs to read and to write a sentence about. (If you pressure the student for time as he picks one of the pair, he may feel even more inclined to write a sentence about a topic he likes.) An item like this, although similar to the previous pairing item, is different in that we are not merely asking the student to say which subject of the two he prefers, we are asking him to do something with the subject. Check your paragraph pairs to make sure there are no great differences between them; they should look alike on the printed page, be about the same length, and be as equally attractive as possible. (For example, if one paragraph contained dialogue and the other didn't, the eye might be quickly drawn to the dialogue. If one paragraph started out, "The early history of . . . ," and if the other began with, "Sex is the key to . . . ," or with, "Excitement is the only word for . . . ," they might be unevenly balanced in terms of attention-getting power. Finding paragraphs that might be suitable is not difficult; ask three or four students to select paragraphs that look about the same when there are no titles on them. The object of the item is to see which topics the student will address himself to when given a choice . . . when all other things are equal except the subject.)

14. On the slips of paper that follow, you are given several pairs of paragraphs. As rapidly as you can, read *one* paragraph from each pair and write one sentence telling what the paragraph is about.

   a.   **Mathematics**   **English**

   The slide rule provides a good check for multiplication, division, and square root. The slide rule is far less useful than a computing machine for most statistical work, but to the person working without a machine it is a valuable aid, especially as a check on other computation.

   The writing of business letters is one of the skills influencing the success of those who work in the business world. Those who write clear, understandable letters are much more likely to receive a favorable response than those whose letters are disorganized, full of strikeovers, or poor grammatically.

b. Science	History of Education
Although it is true that new facts and principles are the result of science they are not science. Science is a process, or collection of processes, through which new information and insight are developed. A scientist is a scientist because of the procedures he follows in the pursuit of knowledge; he is not a scientist because he knows some of the results discovered by others.	It can be argued, then, that the introduction of the textbook into the American university was forced by the student and adjusted to by the administration. Students started many literary societies and read a great variety of books, and they learned from them. Textbooks were eventually introduced into the classroom as an instructional aid, but with resistance from faculty and administration.

How long should a questionnaire be?

Your questionnaire should contain as many items as you feel are necessary to give you good evidence about the existence of approach or avoidance tendencies toward your subject.

Which items should a questionnaire include?

Those that *you* will accept; those that would cause you to make the instructional changes they suggest. Since you are constructing this instrument for your own use, it makes sense to include only those items that you will accept as meaningful. This is not to say you should not be interested in the *validity* of the items. After all, some items are better indicators than others of how a student is likely to behave in certain situations. But as important as the issue of validity is, I believe validity should be secondary to self-acceptance. *First* develop a set of indicators that you would accept, and *then* ask questions about validity. This way, you can get started *now* and refine your procedures as you gather experience and as more information becomes available on validation techniques.

If students know we are asking "attitude" questions, can't they fake their responses? Isn't the student merely going to tell us what he thinks we want to hear?

The honesty with which a student will answer the items on a questionnaire partly depends on how well he trusts the person who is doing the asking. If there is little trust, the student will do his best to give what he thinks are appropriate answers; that is, answers that will do him as little damage as possible. If there is a great deal of trust, the student feels no need to conceal his true opinions and he will be more likely to respond accurately.

Suppose I handed out a tendency questionnaire and said, "I am honestly interested in improving my instruction, and I would like very much to know whether I have succeeded in reaching some of my teaching objectives. I'd appreciate it if you would answer these questions as honestly as you can. Your answers will have nothing whatever to do with your grades." And then suppose I let a small smile turn up the edges of my lips in gleeful anticipation. What would you believe, my words or my lips?

There are any number of ways in which we can say one thing and clearly communicate something entirely different by our actions, but we *can* get reliable responses to questionnaire items if we ask for responses under appropriate conditions— conditions that convince the student that we mean what we say.

If you have been teaching for any length of time, you have probably developed some procedures for administering questionnaires to which there will be only anonymous responses. Perhaps you use items that require checking but no writing. Perhaps you ask a student to collect the papers and shuffle them before handing them to you. These are useful techniques, and you can easily collect others by asking your colleagues. The main thing is to arrange conditions so that the student believes his responses will *in no way reflect on him or his grade*. Convincing him that there is no way in which you can identify his personal responses may be the best way to succeed. Insist that no names be put on papers, ask a student to collect papers and tabulate responses, ask that the questionnaire be answered outside the classroom and turned in to a student, or ask that papers be put into a box like a voter's ballot. Whatever procedure you select should tell the student about your sincerity in learning how you might improve the course.

As for instructions to students, I find that I get better results if I tell them I am trying to improve my instruction than if I tell them I am interested in measuring or assessing their attitudes about my subject. Students seem to be more eager to help in response to the first statement than to the second. I asked some students why this might be so, and their answers led me to conclude that it is because "I want to learn something about your attitudes . . . " still has a hint of student grading in it.

If you decide to administer a questionnaire at the beginning of the course as well as at the end so you can see if there are positive or negative shifts in approach tendencies, I suggest you tell your students their answers will help you make better decisions about how to organize the course and about where to put special emphasis.

Course-related Behaviors

There are several things students are doing, or not doing, about the subject as they go through a course. Some of these actions can be used as additional circumstantial evidence from which to make predictions about future behavior. If you compare observations made during the first third of the course with those made during the last third, you can get a further indication of how approach tendencies may have improved.

The items that follow will give you figures to work with. You may consider your results as evidence of approach or avoidance tendencies. Once again, no single item is expected to be as good a predictor as a combination of items: The more evidence the better. Once again, too, items are for various academic levels.

1. Percentage of students completing the course, or total number of dropouts. (Of course there were good reasons for the dropouts, but the drop speaks louder than the excuse; dropping out is the extreme case of absenteeism.)

2. Total number of students late for class. (Of course they may be late one day because the previous instructor didn't know how to turn himself off . . . or for a million other reasons . . but regular tardiness may be a useful indicator.)

3. Total number of absences. (Industry has been using absenteeism as an indicator of approach tendencies for a long time.)

4. Total number of students choosing to attend an *optional* class session.

5. Number of papers or projects turned in that were *not* assigned or required.

6. Number of papers that were longer than required.

7. Number of papers more thoroughly researched than required.

8. Care with which papers or projects were completed. (You might roughly categorize the products into three classes— neat, average, and sloppy—and keep a record of the number falling into each category.)

9. Number of assignments completed on time.

10. Number of students coming to your office to ask questions or to discuss the subject.

11. Number of students on time for their appointments with you.

12. Number of students electing to sign up for another course in the subject.

13. Number of students responding to a request for volunteers to work on a special subject-related project.

14. Number of unassigned library books taken out on the subject.

15. Amount of money spent by students for books, equipment, or materials relating to the subject. (How many classical records did they buy during the last thirty days of their music appreciation course?)

16. Total number of students active in the club or group organized in pursuit of the subject (math club, French club, etc.).

17. Number of students indicating a desire to "major" in the subject.

If none of these items suits you, and if they don't stimulate you to think of course-related student behavior you *would* accept as a basis for making statements about attitudes, I have two more suggestions:

- Talk to some of your students about some subject *other* than what you are teaching. Ask them how they feel about this other subject; ask them how much time they spend in contact with it; ask them what they intend to do with it in the future.

- Observe another instructor's students and ask yourself what *they* do that leads you to infer a tendency toward or away from the other instructor's subject. *These* are behaviors you *are* willing to use as indicators of approach toward something taught by someone else; they may very well be used as indicators of approach toward your own subject.*

Isn't it possible for an approach tendency to remain negative but still have moved in a positive direction?

Yes, of course it is.

Shouldn't we try to measure the strength of a tendency? Is it enough merely to make a gross assessment of positive and negative?

Yes. It *is* enough *for now*. Let's move ahead one step at a time. Let's first do what we *can* do to send away as many students as possible with feelings on the positive side of the ledger, and then concern ourselves with more refined evaluations of approach strengths. The fault is not in using crude measures, but in doing nothing until perfection comes along.

---

*You will find some additional suggestions for suitable course-related student behavior items in David R. Krathwohl, Benjamin S. Bloom, and Bertram B. Masia, *Taxonomy of Educational Objectives, Handbook II: Affective Domain*, New York: David McKay, Inc., 1964.

A poker player down to his last coins was asked, "How're ya doin'?"

"I dunno," he replied.

"What? You don't know how you're making out?"

"Oh, sure," said the player. "I know how I'm making out, but I don't know how I'm doing it."

10

Improving Results

Sometimes we know how well we are doing, but we don't know exactly how we are doing it. If we knew what we were doing that was contributing to success, and if we knew what we were doing that was contributing to failure, we could do more of the one and less of the other.

As we agreed earlier, there are factors other than the instructor that influence student behavior. There are peers, parents, relatives, and the mass media. This being the case, it isn't realistic to expect that all students will leave your influence anxious to learn more about your subject or to behave enthusiastically at the mention of it. It isn't realistic to feel responsible for all of the negative affect with which your students leave. But should you feel responsible for any of it? How can you find out whether *you* are among the sources of negative influence?

The object of this chapter is to suggest ways to assess the approach-avoidance characteristics of intructional activities, to detect whether avoidance-producing influences may have sneaked onto the scene without your knowing it, and to identify the positive influences that might be strengthened.

The method suggested consists of identifying discrepancies between *principles* of good practice and *actual* practice. This is done by asking a series of questions of your instruction and your instructional environment (1) to determine whether practices that produce aversive conditions and consequences may have inadvertently crept into the classroom and (2) to determine ways in which practices that lead to positive conditions and consequences may be strengthened or emphasized.

This procedure, called an *affect analysis,* for want of a better name, has been developed with the help of some very tolerant teachers. Originally, the procedure was designed to be used while working as a private consultant to teachers interested in achieving the affect objective as well as they might. It has been modified somewhat so that a do-it-yourself version could be offered for your consideration.*

The affect analysis, as originally conducted, consists of two or three periods of classroom observation, interviews of several students who are enrolled in the target course and several who are not, and a review of instructional materials, the immediate environment, and administrative practices. The object of the analysis is to identify conditions and consequences experienced by students when they approach and contact the target subject. This is no less and no more than the practice of diagnosis. When the physician looks at a person to identify ways his health can be improved, the physician first makes an examination . . .

---

*Interaction analysis is a more sophisticated procedure for looking at effects produced by teachers. An excellent reference is E. J. Amidon and J. B. Hough (eds.), *Interaction Analysis: Theory, Research and Application,* Reading, Mass.: Addison-Wesley Publishing Co., Inc., 1967.

collecting information through which he can spot discrepancies between what is and what ought to be. The patient's comments tell him that something is awry (such as "Oh, Doctor, my stomach is awry"), and his analysis of conditions is intended to tell him just what may be causing the difficulty.

The results of the analysis are given to the teacher who asked for it, *and to no one else*. The discussion with the teacher is designed to point out favorable and unfavorable practices, and to discover ways in which the teacher might work around any aversive conditions not under his control.

An example may serve to illustrate the usefulness of this procedure. A fourth grade art teacher was very successful in motivating an interest in art activities. She was liked by her students, and they wanted to be able to do the things she could do. But by mid-semester it became clear that interest in art was declining. Many of the children demonstrated increasing apathy toward art, and began expressing antagonism toward art class (not toward the teacher, but toward "art *class*"). An affect analysis for this teacher revealed the somewhat subtle cause of this situation. In explaining the project for the day, the teacher used between one-fourth to one-half of the class period. Then, just as the children had organized their materials and were hard at work, the bell rang and they had to stop and go on to another classroom.

There was good motivation in this case, and an enthusiastic and skillful teacher. But there was also an event that successfully blocked the motivated activity of the students . . . and frustration resulted. Since frustration is one of the conditions people try to avoid, these students came to associate art class with something unpleasant. Aggravating the situation still further was the fact that the teacher knew time was short, and this caused her to hover over the students while they worked and urge them to work faster.

Once this state of affairs was pointed out to the teacher, there was no need to suggest a solution; making her aware of it was enough. Although she had no control over the length of the period and could not change the administrative rules, she was able to get around the restrictive time allocation by reorganizing her activities so more work time would be available to the students.

The pages that follow will describe a procedure by which you can observe and analyze your own instruction. It isn't possible to be completely objective about ourselves, so you may miss an item or two that might be spotted by a more objective observer. Moreover, some of the conditions that effect approach behavior are a little too subtle to spot singlehandedly, and one or two others may be a little too embarrassing to be visible. That really doesn't matter, however, because the procedure described will allow you to be at least partially able to stand beside yourself or behind yourself (which is a neat trick) and attain a reasonable amount of objectivity.

What To Observe

Observations are confined to school-related conditions that may exist while the student is in the presence of the subject matter, because it is these over which we have most control. Record all conditions you suspect might contribute to the increase or decrease of the student's interest in the subject he is studying. Record all conditions that are in themselves aversive or that might cause an aversive condition to appear.

There are thousands of acts, conditions, and processes that might influence approach and avoidance behaviors, and it would be impossible to list them all here. Some of these conditions and events have a minor effect, and some have major effects. Record those that stand out and those you suspect of being strong enough to have an influence.

There are five areas for observation, but only these four will be considered here:*

---

*The fifth area is that of social environment. It includes those attitude-related conditions generated by students themselves, such as: disrupting or assisting others, ridiculing or applauding the work of others, and demonstrating that contact with the subject is either an 'in" or "out" thing to do. This area can have serious positive or negative influence, and it is excluded from the affect analysis outline only because I cannot talk about social environment analysis from firsthand experience.

- The instructor.
- Instructional materials and devices.
- The physical environment.
- Administrative rules or policies.

There are three categories of questions to answer for each of the areas for observation.

- *Contact Difficulty.* How difficult is it for the student to make contact with the subject? How difficult is it for the student to experience the subject?
- *Contact Conditions.* How difficult is it for the student to stay in the presence of, or in contact with, the subject? What conditions associated with subject matter manipulation make it easy or difficult for the student to continue the activity?
- *Contact Consequences.* What are the consequences of working with the subject? What are the results of the student's attempts to learn and produce in relation to the subject?

On the pages that follow, suggested items for observation are offered in all four observation areas. It is fully recognized, however, that not all of the aversive conditions discovered in the analysis are under the control of the instructor . . . not all can be eliminated or modified by the instructor. Some aversive conditions may be beyond everyone's control. But you can't fix it if you can't find it. To eliminate or alleviate problems, it is first necessary to identify and define them. Once that is accomplished, decisions about appropriate action may be made.

The Instructor

Contact Difficulty. What does the instructor do that makes it easy or difficult for the students to experience the subject?

- Does he speak loud enough for all to hear easily?
- Does he speak clearly?

- Is his vocabulary level consistent with the subject level? (Does he use a freshman vocabulary for freshman subjects, or a senior vocabulary for freshman subjects?)
- Does he continually orient students so that they always know where they are and where they are going?
- Does he specify his objectives clearly? Does he give students written copies of the objectives?
- Does he allow or encourage questions?
- Does he allow or encourage discussion? Does he allow the student to express and develop his own ideas?
- Are students allowed or encouraged to pursue some special interest they may have developed in the subject, or must they all follow the instructor?

Contact Conditions. What does the instructor do to make it easy or difficult to stay in contact with the subject?

- Does he put students to sleep with a monotone?
- Does he read the textbook aloud?
- Does he do little else than lecture?
- Does he ramble?
- How interested or enthused does he appear to be about the subject?
- Must students remain inactive for long periods of time?
- Is he interested in teaching students, or is he more interested in keeping order?
- What happens while students are taking exams? Are they eager to demonstrate their achievement, or are they frightened and anxious?
- Does *he* behave as he wants his students to behave?
- Does he generate discomfort while talking about or presenting the subject? (One college instructor drops cigarette ashes on the students who are forced to sit in the front row. All eyes are on his ash, and it is very difficult to pay attention to the subject.)

Contact Consequences. What happens to the students when they do work with, or manipulate, the target subject?

- How are their questions answered? With interest? With hostility? With insult, ridicule, or disdain? Are they ignored?
- How are student comments or attempts to discuss the subject responded to? Is the student made to feel stupid? Is he encouraged or discouraged by the instructor's responses?
- What happens when a student completes a project? Turns in an assignment?
- Are exam results returned promptly?
- Is student work treated with respect or held up to ridicule?
- Are projects or assignments evaluated promptly? By whom?
- Does the instructor use subject matter as an instrument of punishment?
- Does the instructor insist that assignments be turned in promptly, and then ignore them?
- Does the instructor do anything that convinces the student he could never be competent in the subject? That his best efforts aren't good enough?

Instructional Materials and Devices

Contact Difficulty. Do the materials facilitate or inhibit student contact with the subject?

- Are there materials that help the student work with the subject, or is there nothing more than the instructor's words *about* the subject?
- Do type size and style make it difficult to read the material? (Ask a student.)
- Is the sound quality of audio materials good enough so that students can hear with ease?

- Is the material organized so that the student can easily find what he is looking for? Is it clearly indexed?
- Are the materials easy to get at?
- Can the projectors be operated easily? Extension cord available? Threading easy? Screen handy? Material clearly visible on screen without extensive room-darkening efforts?

Contact Conditions.   How easy or difficult is it to continue to use the materials?

- Are the models in good shape, or do they require pampering to be used?
- Are the films deadly dull?
- Are the texts boring?
- Are the materials relevant?
- Is it easy to see the place or importance of the materials, or do students consider them nuisances?
- What is the reading difficulty? (An introductory text was once prepared by a corporation for use in courses attended by men with a high school education. The text was well illustrated, comprehensive, and attractively bound. Some time after it had been distributed, however, it was found to be far too difficult for the students; the students couldn't get next to the ideas because of the vocabulary. Here was a case of freshman subject matter being taught with graduate school vocabulary. The discrepancy between subject matter level and vocabulary level was "discovered" when it was found that at least one group of instructors had written *another* text designed to teach the students to understand the *introductory* text.)
- What is the viewing difficulty?
- What is the hearing difficulty?

Contact Consequences.   What is the result of using the course materials?

- Do students have eyestrain or headaches after difficult reading or viewing?
- Do students suffer from "relevance confusion"? Do they come away wondering why the materials were used?
- Are they exasperated or frustrated because of equipment malfunction?
- Are they frustrated because they had to watch while other students performed the experiments, made the adjustments, or took the measurements?

The Physical Environment

Contact Conditions. How does the physical environment make it difficult or easy for the student to experience the subject?

- Is the room too large for students in the back to see well?
- Does room shape make it difficult for some to see over the heads of others?
- Does lack of wall space minimize subject matter displays?
- How are the acoustics?
- How good is the lighting?
- Does the student have adequate work space?
- Is student work space relatively comfortable? Or uncomfortable enough to prove distracting?
- Does the seating arrangement facilitate distraction?
- Is the noise level reasonable?
- Is the environment generally too cold? Too hot? Too stuffy?

Contact Consequences. Would the student's world *improve* as a result of *leaving* the environment in which he was closeted with the subject?

- Is the student anxious to get away from the environment?
- Is the student relieved when he leaves the environment? Why?

Administrative Rules or Policies

Contact Difficulty. Are there rules that make it difficult for the student to approach the subject?

- Is the instructor accessible to the students when needed?
- Does distance get between the student and the subject? How far does he have to travel between classroom and laboratory? Between classrooms?
- Are materials accessible to the student when he needs them?
- Is the library open when the student is free to use it?
- Are library books easily accessible to the student, or does the librarian stand between the student and the books?
- How much paper work (form-filling) stands between the student and library books?
- How much administrative procedure stands between the instructor and course materials?
- Are projectors permanently available where the student can use them?
- Are films and filmstrips permanently available where the student can use them?
- Are students allowed to operate equipment?
- Are visuals permanently available where the instructor uses them?
- What proportion of a laboratory period does the student spend in setting up and taking down experiments? In signing out and signing in?
- What proportion of the laboratory period does the student spend making calculations, or doing other things that could as easily be done elsewhere?
- Does the instructor insist on checking every step of the student's work before he is allowed to proceed?
- What conditions exist that might discourage students from operating equipment and using materials?

Contact Conditions. Do the rules make it difficult for the student to stay in contact with the subject?

- Are all students made to proceed at the same rate?
- Are brighter students prevented from "getting ahead" of slower students?
- Are slower students given more time to understand the subject and to achieve than other students?
- Are students to turn off their interest in one subject when a rigid time block ends (the bell rings) and turn on their interest in another subject? In other words, must student interest conform to administrative policy, or does policy encourage students to work with a subject until *they* reach a stopping point?
- Are classes frequently interrupted by announcements over a PA system or by other intrusions?
- Are students of considerably differing abilities paired, causing boredom to the faster and frustration or embarrassment to the slower?
- What conditions exist that make it difficult for the instructor to maintain interest in his students and in his subject?
- Is the instructor overloaded with busywork?
- Does the instructor have to give the same presentation more than twice?

Contact Consequences. Does administrative policy reward or punish the student for his efforts?

- If a student finishes his work earlier than the others, is he made to sit still until others finish or until the period is over? Is his diligence followed by some other form of unpleasant consequence, such as cleaning chores or "make work" assignments?
- Are grades related to student achievement in relation to course objectives, or to how well the student's peers happen to have performed? In other words, is evaluation based on objective-related performance?

- What kinds of recognition or privileges are there for student achievement?

- Do administrators hand out as many rewards as they do punishments? (Does the principal call as many students to his office for *good* performance as he does for *poor* performance?)

- For what kinds of performance does the administration reward the instructors? Are instructors rewarded on the basis of their interest in, and efforts on behalf of, students? Are instructors rewarded on the basis of the amount of student behavior they have changed? Or are they rewarded mostly for committee work, publications, and PTA attendance?

- Does administrative policy *allow* successful teachers to be rewarded more than unsuccessful teachers?

- Does administrative policy reward unsuccessful teaching by taking from the classroom those students with whom the teacher has failed and giving them to specialists to work with in special rooms?

- What do administrators *do* to identify how well each instructor is performing?

Each of the questions posed will provide a clue to one or more condition possibly operating to depress subject-matter interest. They are by no means all the questions to ask, and do not identify all the things to look for. They provide a guide to get you started, and will, hopefully, remind you of other factors to check on.

While reading through the questions you may have had your doubts about the way they were organized . . . you may feel that one or more items should come under a different heading. Put them there. The object of the checklist is not to provide a neat classification system . . . the object is to provide an aid to the analysis of instructional effects.

How To Observe

1. Record one or two of your class sessions. Though video-taping is preferable because it provides more information, an audio recording is better than nothing. If your course has lab sessions, record one or two of them, too.

2. Play back the recordings in private while considering the questions listed on pages 87-94. Try to assume you are looking or listening to recordings taken in someone else's class. There is no need to get elaborate about the notes you take. After all, you are looking for clues to ways of increasing the percentage of approach responses, not in collecting data for a journal article. So keep it simple.

3. Spend some time looking over the materials used in the course. Inspect the texts, films, project materials, and anything else that is used during instruction. If the student is expected to operate such equipment as slide projectors, tape recorders, etc., operate them yourself while asking the suggested questions.

4. Consider administrative policies in relation to their effect on the student. Consider the time of day that students study the subject, the length of the period, the difficulty of getting to the class from the previous one, administrative interruptions, and administrative rules that may affect approach.

5. Talk with a few of your students with a view toward checking the observations you have made during the previous steps. The students are the ones being influenced and, although their self-knowldege isn't perfect, their comments about their reactions are better than your guesses. If it is at all possible, talk with a few of the students who have completed the course under consideration. They may have a better idea about the durability of the effect of conditions that influence their interest.

Acting on Observations

What is the most aversive condition or consequence you have discovered? Is it under your direct control? If it is under your control, try to reduce or eliminate it. If it isn't under your control, it might be useful to bring the condition to the attention of the appropriate person. If the condition is not under your control and you judge it to be so much a part of the current system that you would have no chance of influencing it, it probably wouldn't help to mention it to anyone. Instead, try to find a way of working around it or minimizing it. For example, the aversive affects of an uncomfortable physical environment can be reduced by allowing students more freedom of movement.

Imagine that the notes you have taken are the results of an analysis of someone else's course and that you are going to summarize for him the best and the worst of his instructional situation. Check those items in your notes. They are the items with which you should concern yourself. Ignore the rest. It is not easy to change, even for good causes; you are more likely to succeed if you concentrate on one item at a time.

It may come to pass that a colleague will ask you to help him with an affect analysis of his instruction and instructional environment. If this happens, and you accept, you have an obligation to report to him, *and to no one else.* You should consider that you have contracted a client-counselor relationship; keep all results in the deepest confidence. If the person for whom you have made the observations wants to tell others about them . . . that is his prerogative . . . but it is not yours. In accepting a request to make observations and collect information, you agree to do just that—to make observations and collect information. It is highly inappropriate to pass judgment on your results by communicating it to others. Remember the wisdom that stems from the comment about casting the first stone, and about glass houses. Discretion is essential.

If you have never performed as a consultant before, one further word of caution is in order. Though your observations will be aimed at conditions relating to approach or avoidance, you will observe other things as well. You may very well observe events, procedures, or content not consistent with your own notions of effective instruction. Although it is inevitable that you *will* make such observations . . . *leave them alone.* Do not record them, do not talk about them, and do not report them to the person for whom you are observing. Even though this person has asked you to tell him about anything you think may be improved, it is unwise to take him at his word. He is no more exempt from the laws of behavior than you or I, and one of the best ways of turning yourself into an aversive stimulus that he will tend to avoid is to inundate him with criticism. Tell him only about the conditions that may be affecting approach and avoidance behavior toward the subject. None of us likes to hear about our weaknesses . . . so be objective . . . and above all, be gentle. Do unto others . . . .

Summing Up

Our success in influencing future performance is in part a function of our success at sending students away with tendencies to approach, rather than avoid, the things we want them to think about, feel about, and do about.

How can we improve our chances of strengthening approach?

- By making sure there are as few aversive conditions present as possible while the student is in the presence of the subject we are teaching him.
- By making sure that the student's contact with the subject is followed by positive, rather than aversive, consequences.
- By modeling the very kind of behavior we would like to see exhibited by our students.

How can we identify conditions and consequences that are attractive or aversive?

- By learning what we can about principles of behavior and about how to recognize their application in the world around us.

- By conducting an affect analysis to find ways of improving the match between what we do and what these principles suggest that we do.

How can we measure our success at strengthening approach?

- By identifying as many observable behaviors as possible that we would accept as evidence of approach tendency.
- By comparing the percentage, or frequency, of approach responses to our subject when the student arrives with that recorded when he leaves.

Epilogue

It is easy to teach hate . . . anywhere in the world you look there is evidence of that. As a species, we do not seem to lack skill in teaching each other to avoid people of other colors, of other ideas, of other religions, and those who might have been born in this country or that. Perhaps there is something about us that makes this inevitable . . . perhaps we are not yet ready for a massive anti-hate program . . . perhaps we are not yet civilized enough, or strong enough, to apply what is already known in preventing further spread of aversion. Perhaps it isn't realistic to believe we are ready to try to stamp out the game of "you name it and I'll teach you to avoid it."

Perhaps.

Be that as it may, those with the responsibility for influencing the behavior of others cannot accept such a defeatist position. To be a professional means to accept responsibility . . . responsibility for actions and for results. It is to act in the best interests of those served . . . to help them grow rather than shrivel. When we accept the reponsibility for professionally influencing the lives and actions of other people, we must do all we can to make that influence positive rather than negative. When we accept the money and the trust of the community, we must accept not only the responsibility for sending our students away with as much knowledge and skill as is within our power to give them, but also for sending them away with the ability and the inclination to use those skills to help themselves and others.

There are enough aversion-producing instruments in this old world of ours. As professional instructors, we must not let it be said that *we* are among them.

A Time for Tribute

"Help, help," I cried.

And did they ever!

As you might guess, a book about approach tendencies ought to trigger approach responses toward the subject of approach responses. Accordingly, *Developing Attitude Toward Learning* was formulated in two loose stages. The first stage consisted of telling the content to teachers, individually and in groups, and noting their reactions, comments, and suggestions. The object was to find out what it took to get them nodding and to keep them nodding all the way through.

The second stage began when the content was in written form. It consisted mainly of asking teachers and colleagues who tested the various drafts to mark anything that slowed them down, turned them off, or rubbed them the wrong way; to describe what might have caused them to back off; and, finally, to describe what might have caused them to move forward.

And did they ever!

They made me change the sequence of topics until it made sense to *them*, and showed no respect whatever for what was "logical" to *me*; ripped out paragraphs I was very fond of and trampled them into oblivion; caused the demise of clever explanations that nobody seemed to understand; bludgeoned me into burning a long chapter (indeed!) on the development of affective objectives and half of one on the statistics of attitude assessment (nobody cared); and vetoed examples that didn't examp.

Such impudence cannot go unpunished; such ego batterers must be exposed to public view. Therefore, with ropes of gratitude I tie to the pillory of immortality the thirty teachers who attended the workshop sponsored by the London County Council (1963), the twenty teachers who attended a workshop sponsored by the University of Buffalo (1966), the nine graduate student-teachers of the University of Rochester (1966), and these more recent culprits, who made marks all over my neat pages: Albert Bandura; Bruce Bergum; Edith Bryant; David Cram; Anne Dreyfuss; Sister Charlene Foster, S.N.D. de Namur; Arthur Hyatt; Jane Kilkenny; Leon Lessinger; Richard Lewis; Jeanne Mager; Mike Nisos; Judy Opfer; Peter Pipe; Maryjane Rees; Charles Selden; Nancy Selden; Caroline Smiley; Margaret Steen; James Straubel; Walter Thorne; and Jack Vaughn.

Selected References

The procedures described in *Developing Attitude Toward Learning* are derived from those referred to as *behavior modification and contingency management*. The following references describe the theory and practice of many of these techniques:

BANDURA, A. "Behavioral Psychotherapy," *Scientific American*, No. 216 (1967), pp. 78-86.

_____. "Social Learning Through Imitation," in M. R. Jones (ed.), *Nebraska Symposium on Motivation: 1962*. Lincoln, Nebr.: University of Nebraska Press, 1962, pp 211-269.

BANDURA, A., and WALTERS, R. H. *Social Learning and Personality Development*. New York: Holt, Rinehart & Winston, Inc., 1963.

ULLMAN, L. P., and KRASNER, L. *Case Studies in Behavior Modification*. New York: Holt, Rinehart & Winston, Inc., 1965, 401 pages.

ULRICH, R.; STACHNIK, T.; and MABRY, J. *Control of Human Behavior*. Glenview, Ill.: Scott, Foresman & Co., 1966, 349 pages.

For additional information about procedures that might be useful for measuring approach tendency or attitude, the following are recommended:

KRATHWOHL, D. R.; BLOOM, B. S.; and MASIA, B. B. *Taxonomy of Educational Objectives, Handbook II: Affective Domain*. New York: David McKay, Inc., 1964.

OPPENHEIM, A. N. *Questionnaire Design and Attitude Measurement.* New York: Basic Books, Inc., 1966, 298 pages.

OSGOOD, C. E.; SUCI, G. J.; and TANNENBAUM, P. H. *The Measurement of Meaning.* Urbana, Ill.: University of Illinois Press, 1957, 342 pages.

WEBB, E. J.; CAMPBELL, D. T.; SCHWARTZ, R. D.; and SECHREST, L. *Unobtrusive Measures: Nonreactive Research in the Social Sciences.* Chicago: Rand McNally & Co., 1966, 225 pages.

These references contain useful information regarding further procedures for the analysis of instruction:

AMIDON, E. J., and HOUGH, J. B., (eds.). *Interaction Analysis: Theory, Research and Application.* Reading, Mass.: Addison-Wesley Publishing Co., Inc., 1967, 402 pages.

SPINDLER, G. D. *Education and Culture.* New York: Holt, Rinehart & Winston, Inc., 1964, 571 pages.

370.15
M19

LINCOLN CHRISTIAN UNIVERSITY

34073

3 4711 00209 1066